CLASSIC
TV WESTERNS

CLASSIC

TV WESTERNS
A PICTORIAL HISTORY

RONALD JACKSON

A CITADEL PRESS BOOK
Published by Carol Publishing Group

A Citadel Press Book
Published by Carol Publishing Group
Citadel Press is a registered trademark of Carol Communications, Inc.
Editorial Offices: 600 Madison Avenue, New York, N.Y. 10022
Sales and Distribution Offices: 120 Enterprise Avenue, Secaucus, N.J. 07094
In Canada: Canadian Manda Group, P.O. Box 920, Station U, Toronto, Ontario M8Z 5P9
Queries regarding rights and permissions should be addressed to Carol Publishing Group, 600 Madison Avenue, New York, N.Y. 10022

Carol Publishing Group books are available at special discounts for bulk purchases, sales promotions, fund raising, or educational purposes. Special editions can be created to specifications. For details, contact Special Sales Department, Carol Publishing Group, 120 Enterprise Avenue, Secaucus, N.J. 07094

Designed by A. Christopher Simon

Manufactured in the United States of America

10 9 8 7 6 5 4 3 2 1

LIBRARY OF CONGRESS CATALOGING-IN-PUBLICATION DATA
Jackson, Ronald, 1947–
    Classic TV westerns : a pictorial history / by Ronald Jackson.
        p.   cm. — (Citadel Press film series)
    "A Citadel Press book."
    ISBN 0-8065-1486-8 (pbk.)
    1. Westerns (Television programs)—United States—History and criticism.   2. Westerns (Television programs)—United States—History and criticism—Pictorial works.   I. Title. II. Series.
PN1992.8.W4J23   1994
791.43'6278—dc20   93-45775
                                                                          CIP

This book is dedicated with love
to my wife *NARLENE*
and
my mother *ARTIE JACKSON*

ACKNOWLEDGMENTS

Many thanks to the people who helped in the compilation of this book.

Athena Alvarez, American Broadcasting Company, Arness Productions, Arthur Ashton, Claire Ashton, Buddy Barnett, Gene Barry, Bonnie Bee, Marilyn Bieler, Mark Bishop, Sarah Blemel, Eddie Brandt, Ed & Willery Capron, Cinema Collectors, Columbia Broadcasting Systems, Chuck Connors, Lee Corman, Daystar Productions, Billy Deaton, Desilu Productions, Bob Diverde, Scott Domnie, Claude Dume, Doug & Betsy Dunman, Empire Publishing, Bruce Fertel, John Field, Oscard FIFI, Filmation Associates, Four Star Productions, Fox Network, David Garcia, Jess Garcia, Kurt Gardner, Barry Goldberg, Ron & Ann Greenwood, Rose M. Grumley, Hollywood Collector's Bookstore, Will Hutchins, Independent Television Productions, Peter & Nancy IsQuick, Esther Jackson, Joseph Koch, Charlie Lamb, Elizabeth B. Laskoski, Bert Laszlo, Jack MacFadden, Jock Mahoney, Ron Mandelbaum, Mark VII LTD., Bryce Martin, David Miller, Milton T. Moore, Movie Star News, National Broadcasting Company, Bob & Diane New, Arvo Ojala, Jerry Ohlinger's Movie Material, Overland Productions, Buck Owens, Photofest, Revue Productions, Dale Robertson, Roy Rogers & Dale Evans, John Russell, Stephen Sally, Peter Sawyer, Screen Gems Productions, Jim Sheperd, Richelle Sims, Wayne Stubbs, Thousand Oaks Library, 20th Century Fox Television, TV Guide, Universal Television, Joey Vance, Walt Disney Studios, Warner Brothers Studios, Mary Lou Wigley, Allan J. Wilson, Wyatt Earp Enterprises, ZIV Television Productions, and special thanks to Narlene Capron Jackson.

CONTENTS

CLASSIC
TV WESTERNS

INTRODUCTION

Television Westerns began in the late forties, essentially reworking in half-hour formats of popular cowboy movies—*Hopalong Cassidy*, *The Lone Ranger*, *The Cisco Kid*—and those with Roy Rogers, Gene Autry, "Wild" Bill Elliott, and others. Although the medium was television, the origin of a viewer's interest was, of course, the movies. The content and values of these Westerns were a far cry from the popular war pictures of the 1940s, such as *Back to Bataan*, *Objective, Burma! Destination Tokyo*, or *Guadalcanal Diary*, designed to keep our patriotism and enthusiasm at a high level. Westerns, conversely, were a return to those years of innocence that had once been enjoyed and unfortunately ended with Pearl Harbor. Westerns replaced the "real life" or the "real world" that was depicted in war movies. It was a time to temporarily forget about bombs, bloodshed, death, and dying. Westerns, a typical American genre, helped us maintain a higher standard of patriotism and pride in our great country without the trauma associated with World War II; we took to the cowboys with great relief.

In the beginning we saw the singing cowboys Roy Rogers and Gene Autry, who were role models for kids and adults as well. Regardless of age, every household member clearly understood the message these Westerns were trying to say: the good guys always win and the bad guys always lose in the end. Roy and Gene will most likely be remembered as the first classic Western heroes, while still other television Westerns will never be anything less than great classics, shows like *Bonanza*, *Gunsmoke*, *Maverick*, *The Rifleman*, and *The Lone Ranger*. There are more than 120 classic television Westerns illustrated in this book. Many of these shows have not been seen since they were first aired, but neither have they been forgotten. There were many other great Westerns not covered in this book due to the difficulty in defining certain shows as Westerns rather than adventure series, as in the case of *Hawkeye—The Last of the Mohicans* and *Northwest Passage*, whose settings were in the 1750s. Not all Westerns on television showed cowboys on horseback with a Colt .45 in his holster living in Wyoming. Most Westerns were set during the Civil War period to the modern era. It is evident Westerns are making a comeback, judging from the success of *Young Guns*, Clint Eastwood's *Unforgiven*, and Kevin Costner's *Dances With Wolves* to *Geronimo* and *Tombstone* of 1993, and TV miniseries like *Centennial*, *Son of Morning Star*, *Lonesome Dove*, and *Return to Lonesome Dove*. New television Westerns kicking up the ratings in the 1990s include *The Adventures of Brisco County, Jr.*; *Dr. Quinn, Medicine Woman*; *Harts of the West*; and *Walker, Texas Ranger*, while other new guns of the West are loading up. Let's hope they bring plenty of ammunition and supplies for the seasons to come.

FOREWORD

I remember when I was a small boy, approximately seven or eight years old and growing up in Beattyville, Kentucky, my mother bought our *first* television set. This was sometime around 1954 or 1955. Like all kids, I became mesmerized, my eyes glued to the TV. While most my age were hooked on cartoons or baseball, I was fascinated by the Westerns—*Cheyenne*, *Gunsmoke*, *Wyatt Earp*, and others. There was a certain fixation about Westerns that kept me anticipating the next gunfight, the next saloon brawl, the next bank robbery—events where the good guys stepped in to save the day. Maybe it was the cowboys themselves, their fast guns or their faithful steeds, but growing up I could tell you everything you would want to know about any series or particular episodes. I knew the guns, the gimmicks, the theme songs, the cast and their wardrobe, even down to their spurs. I am not saying I didn't enjoy other television shows. In fact, I hardly missed an episode of *The Untouchables*, *Peter Gunn*, *77 Sunset Strip*, or *Highway Patrol*, but the cowboys were still my heroes. I couldn't wait until Sunday night when *Maverick*, *Lawman*, *The Rebel*, and *Colt .45* kept the television screen smoking. My mother was a big Western fan also, so I never had a problem getting to watch these shows.

Being an only child and a loner, I learned to entertain myself acting out the Western characters and playing their roles. My bicycle was my horse, and my mother made me a cowboy outfit just like the ones I saw on television. I learned to twirl toy guns and outdraw any kid in the hills of Kentucky. I captured many a crook and rustled many a dogie. When I was growing up, kids my age saved books and photos of their favorite movie or television stars. I would tear out every magazine photo of my favorites and paste them in my scrapbook, mostly the television Western stars. I kept every *TV Guide* issue, comic book, and movie-star book. During an interview several years ago with Will Hutchins, we were browsing through many of his photos, looking for the right one to fit the format of this project. I reminded him of several occasions when as a boy I had written to him asking for photos from his popular Western *Sugarfoot*. He was always co-operative in keeping my image of him as a hero by promptly sending me pictures. My mother would give me fifty cents a week for school-lunch money, which I would hide under our house until I had enough to order four-by-five or eight-by-ten glossy photos of the television cowboys. They were a dime each, and that was a large amount of money for a school kid. Movie magazines were a quarter and comic books a dime. The photos were beautiful, most of them taken with large-format cameras—four by five or eight by ten graphic cameras, with the studios taking their time in making publicity shots. A vast number of these negatives and transparencies were destroyed or lost to former employees of the studios and ended up in the hands of hard-core collectors who demand a fortune for them now. Many of the photos in this book are rare and no longer available.

In compiling *Classic TV Westerns*, and throughout my entertainment career, I have been proud to have had the pleasure of interviewing and working with many of my favorite television stars. Perhaps some of my favorite memories were working with "The Duke," John Wayne; playing the banjo with Roy Rogers and

Dale Evans singing "Happy Trails;" and talking to people who were always close to the phone when I needed them—Chuck Connors, Jock Mahoney, and John Russell, who have all passed on. These cowboys have gone on to the great roundup in the sky, but they left a trail of memories that will last forever. We miss you Duke, Lucas, Yancy, and Marshal Troop.

Looking back at my years as a boy watching my small-screen heroes, playing cowboys, and starting my collection of television photos, I somehow knew I would one day put together this book. It is my hope you will receive as much enjoyment from these memories of the Westerns to the viewing of the current ones as I have had in making this book possible.

Ronald Jackson

James Drury of *The Virginian*

Dan Blocker, Michael Landon, Lorne Greene

CHAPTER ONE

THE GUNS OF TELEVISION

In television's early days, starting around 1948, came fun Westerns such as *Hopalong Cassidy*, followed by *The Lone Ranger*, *The Cisco Kid*, *The Gene Autry Show*, and *The Roy Rogers Show*—a trend toward shows about the Old West geared mostly to children. These cowboys were the heroes—role models for today's adults. Many lessons were taught in these shows, one being the bad guy always loses in the end. Every season more and more Westerns seemed to appear, adding to television's fall schedule, and the viewers couldn't get enough of the cowboys. Many other kid-oriented Westerns—*Wild Bill Hickok*, *Rin Tin Tin*, *The Adventures of Kit Carson*, *The Range Rider*, and *Annie Oakley*—were firing away by the mid-fifties. These shows paved the way for adult Westerns reaching a more mature audience. The story line changed somewhat, dealing with real-life struggles and hardships, sufferings relating to alcohol, religion, or other encounters that hit home. It wasn't that the kid Westerns were not good shows—they were, teaching us many of life's principles and values. Adult Westerns, on the other hand, sometimes went far beyond wholesome entertainment, portraying too much violence.

The so-called adult Western began in 1955 with the likes of *Gunsmoke*, *The Life and Legend of Wyatt Earp*, and *Cheyenne*. Television had begun changing during this period, adding new life to the Western interest. There were more than twenty-five Westerns weekly on television by the fall of 1957. These new cowboys were keeping home families who had been moviegoers for decades; instead, the audiences were tuned in to Bret Maverick and Cheyenne Bodie. The film industry was

Ward Bond

17

Wayde Preston

Henry Fonda

on the decline, and the B movie was vanishing. Hollywood producers knew little about television, except that it seemed to be the way to go. Television Westerns were now where they were focusing their cameras. Jack Warner, president of Warner Brothers, struck a groundbreaking deal with ABC Television in 1955 and brought in his son-in-law, William T. Orr, to produce television Westerns for the network, such as *Cheyenne*, *Maverick*, *Colt .45*, *Sugarfoot*, *Lawman*, *Bronco*, and *The Alaskans*.

Four Star Productions rounded up cowboys for CBS Television beginning with *Dick Powell's Zane Grey Theatre*, *Trackdown*, *Wanted: Dead or Alive*, and *Johnny Ringo*. Four Star also produced Westerns for ABC: *The Rifleman*, *Stagecoach West*, and *The Big Valley*. NBC then kept the guns blazing with hit after

James Arness

Steve McQueen

hit: *Tales of Wells Fargo*, *Bat Masterson*, *Bonanza*, *Laramie*, *Law of the Plainsman*, *Wagon Train*, and *The Virginian*. And CBS, of course, had *Gunsmoke*.

In prime years, there were no less than eight Western shows each week being aired, with this number peaking to thirty-two between 1958 and 1961. By 1965, the average had dropped back to eight weekly, and the networks began losing audiences and interest. Then, in the 1980s, came the cable stations, eager for fare to entice a nostalgic audience, and they began rerunning

Gene Barry

19

many classic television Western favorites like *Broken Arrow*, *Bonanza*, *Gunsmoke*, and *The Big Valley*. One thing for certain, however, is that these great series will continue to live in reruns, videos, magazines, as tourist attractions, and in the growing market of Western memorabilia. We can be proud of our heroes in television history, even if nearly all of them were fictional. The author has only one regret in assembling this book, which is that John Wayne never did a television Western.

The Warner Bros. stable of TV westerns featured Wayde Preston *(Colt .45)*, Ty Hardin *(Bronco)*, Jack Kelly *(Maverick)*, John Russell *(Lawman)*, James Garner *(Maverick)*, Peter Brown *(Lawman)*, and Will Hutchins *(Sugarfoot)*.

Will Hutchins of *Sugarfoot*, Peter Brown of *Lawman*, Jack Kelly of *Maverick*, Ty Hardin of *Bronco*, James Garner of *Maverick*, Wayde Preston of *Colt .45,* and John Russell of *Lawman*.

Warner Brothers Studio

CHAPTER TWO

TROUBLE IN DODGE

Westerns were shooting up the small screen on all channels during the late 1950s, but the good guys and the bad guys, the heroes and the varmints, and even the Indians were getting restless. The heroes were soon firing at their makers instead of the villains. Warner Brothers in Burbank, California, began to have contract problems with its top cowboys, causing major walkouts.

Many of these television cowboys were greenhorns in the Hollywood West and had never been near a horse, not to mention rope cattle or shoot a six-gun. On the other hand, some were real cowpokes from Wyoming, Texas, Oklahoma, and Arizona. When it came to business, it didn't matter where they rode in from; it still meant one thing—money.

Becoming a star playing cowboys and Indians was a lot of fun, but that all began to change when the pay became less than the fun. The cowboys began riding off into the sunset by horsepower instead of on horses—one of the first being a Western hero from Laramie, Wyoming: Wayde Preston, star of the *Colt .45* series. Preston began to complain about many problems with the studio, including a low salary with minimal raises, and he probably was justified in doing so. The movie industry was at a low, as were the pay scales in those days. Today the star of a television series can earn up to several hundred thousand dollars per week; whereas, in 1957, Wayde Preston was earning $400 weekly as Christopher Colt on the hit series. Preston, like many of the Western stars, had never acted before signing an exclusive contract to play the lead role of a television series. He was discovered while sitting next to a talent scout during a flight to Los Angeles in 1956. Wayde presented the perfect image

for the lead role: 6′5″ tall with a rugged voice and handsome good looks. Also in his favor was the fact he was a real bareback bronc rider from Wyoming. Preston's problems soon took a toll that ended his career as a leading star. He was a maverick who would not play by Warners' rules and having been independent in his former jobs couldn't adjust to being told what to do and when. After signing a seven-year Warner contract, Preston claimed he'd been ambushed. What he didn't know was how the studio planned to use him, and his distrust and resentment of the industry kept building up to the point of a walkout which ended his career.

In 1958, Preston holstered his Colts following a dispute over the filming of a scene that called for his character, Chris Colt, to climb on top of a moving stagecoach while shooting at the bad guys. He refused, saying that that was a stunt and should be done by a stuntman. William T. Orr, the show's producer, disagreed, insisting he was needed for a close-up camera shot. Wayde walked off the Warner filming lot, got into his car, drove away, and never came back. That was the last time they ever saw Wayde Preston.

Soon after that, Clint Walker, star of ABC's *Cheyenne*, walked out of his contract with Warner Brothers, setting off a long, bitter feud. Walker claimed he was tired of the same old scripts, shooting the "same old Indian," and toiling on the same low salary. The popular 6′6″ Cheyenne Bodie wanted a better piece of the action and was planning a move back to Illinois if the studio did not meet his demands. Warner refused, knowing that if the studio gave in to Walker, other top cowboy stars like James Garner of *Maverick* and Will Hutchins of *Sugarfoot* would put down their guns and pick up their pens and contracts to negotiate a new deal. Clint Walker was replaced by Ty Hardin to play Bronco Layne in the *Cheyenne* series. This change, of course, upset the fans, and the mail poured into the network insisting on the real Cheyenne. In February 1959, Walker managed to settle his dispute with the studio and returned to his famous role as Cheyenne Bodie. Ty Hardin left *Cheyenne* and became the star of his own series, *Bronco*.

In 1960, the walkouts continued; this time James Garner of *Maverick* laid down his cards and was at loggerheads with Warner Brothers. Garner had become a hit almost overnight in this popular television Western, but he too got tangled up in a contract dispute, this time during a writers' strike. The studio refused to let Garner work elsewhere. He filed suit against Warners' for breach of contract, claiming the studio was still active. Warners claimed there was a shortage of scripts during the strike and was not liable for such encounters. Nevertheless, a Los Angeles judge ruled in Garner's favor in 1960, saying Garner could no longer be held to his contract. Another winning hand for the lucky Bret Maverick, however, since Warner Brothers held no animosity toward Garner for the lawsuit. In fact, he returned to Warner in 1978 to play Bret Maverick once again in its TV movie, *The New Maverick*.

Clint Walker of *Cheyenne*

Arvo Ojala

CHAPTER THREE

HOLLYWOOD GUN COACH

Arvo Ojala came to Hollywood, California, in the early 1950s from the Yakima Valley of Washington State. His interest in television and movie Westerns became more than a dream, they became his life. No one knew more about the Old West or being fast on the trigger of a Colt .45 single-action army revolver than Arvo Ojala. Ojala has been recognized as the fastest gunslinger in the world because of his lightning-draw technique. During the 1950s every motion picture studio was sending Ojala their major movie stars for special training from the master. Some of these Rhinestone Cowboys like Frank Sinatra, Robert Redford, Kirk Douglas, Audie Murphy, and Rory Calhoun knew absolutely nothing about fanning, twirling, or shooting a six-gun.

Ojala's unique leather gunbelt-and-holster patented design became almost status symbols to every leading player. James Arness of *Gunsmoke* and Hugh O'Brian of *The Life and Legend of Wyatt Earp* were the first Western heroes to wear the Ojala brand on television. Perhaps the most famous Ojala gunbelt known in television Westerns was Paladin's rig in *Have Gun, Will Travel* in which Richard Boone played the lead. It was a black holster with a silver horsehead chess piece located on the side, used to denote the Knight as Paladin's trademark.

Arvo Ojala has appeared in many movie and television Westerns during a long career, but one memorable scene stands out among the rest. In the dramatic opening of *Gunsmoke* where Marshal Matt Dillon walks out into the street of Dodge City for a showdown gunfight, Dillon's opponent is Ojala.

The Western trend kept Arvo busy serving as technical director on such television series as *Maverick*, *Lawman*, *Cheyenne*, *Sugarfoot*, and *Colt .45.* His extensive knowledge of the history of the Old West amply qualified him to recognize perfection of a script involv-

Arvo Ojala

ing gunplay. Sometimes the leading star wasn't always convincing enough with his fast on the draw to live up to his image during a gunfight. The director would dub in a close-up of Ojala's lightning hand draw. Of course, when the scene required live ammunition, Arvo was there to stand in and make the hero shine in performance. In an interview with the author of this book, Arvo stated, "One of my most enthusiastic and astute disciples was the late singer and actor, Sammy Davis, Jr., who guest-starred as a gunslinger on such Westerns as *Lawman* and *The Rifleman*."

Currently, Arvo is working with cowboys wearing the Ojala gunbelts in the new movie *Maverick,* starring Mel Gibson and James Garner. The brand is also being worn in *The Adventures of Brisco County, Jr*.

When we look back at those halcyon days of the 1950s and 1960s, some questions come to mind; would these Western cliffhangers have been as great without John Wayne, Roy Rogers, and Gene Autry? Would television Westerns have been as spectacular minus the Cartwrights, the Mavericks, Marshal Matt Dillon, or Lucas McCain? Perhaps the last question is, would these Western heroes have been as memorable without their unique trademark costumes and leathercrafts by artisans like Arvo Ojala or Ed Bolin, another famous gunbelt designer who created the fancy double-holster rigs worn by Clayton Moore (*The Lone Ranger*), Roy Rogers and others. Nevertheless, this great era in movie and television history will never be forgotten because that is when the West was the best.

UNSOLD PILOTS

Westerns! Westerns! And more Westerns! Cowboys came from New York; they came from Los Angeles; some even came from England; but during the 1950s we accepted anything and everything that looked like a cowboy. The cowboys and the Indians dominated those years. Cowpokes with their fancy guns, their horses, and beautiful women. It was a craze of the West for television. The studios and actors were kept busy making new Westerns. Many pilot shows filmed to sell a Western project to a sponsor or network often never got past the screening room. It is uncertain how many potentially great Western shows were shelved or destroyed during the stampede. The studios couldn't load their cameras fast enough to shoot for another *Maverick* or *Gunsmoke*. Screen stars like John Payne, Henry Fonda, Dale Robertson, Barry Sullivan, and Audie Murphy were trying to make a transition from the big screen to television when the motion picture industry reached a record low. Many of those leading players did not make the move to television simply because there was not enough airtime for more Westerns. Movie cowboys of the B-Western era were making pilots trying to sell their guns to a new television audience.

Cowboy star William Boyd bought the rights to his movie character, *Hopalong Cassidy*, and sold *The Hopalong Cassidy Show* to television in 1949 as its first Western. The following year came *The Lone Ranger*, starring Clayton Moore. Roy Rogers and Dale Evans rode in with *The Roy Rogers Show*, and staying in the saddle for a new television series was cowboy star Gene Autry in *The Gene Autry Show*. While many Western heroes survived television, others did not. Take "Wild" Bill Elliott, one of the B Western's most beloved cowboys. In 1950, Elliott filmed a pilot for television called *The Marshal of Trail City*, which was never sold. In 1957, Elliott made another pilot for a possible television series entitled *El Coyote*. It too was shot down. Cowboy star Rex Allen was to head a television series in 1959, *Mister Cowboy*, but it too never materialized. Among other unsold pilots during the 1950s were such shows as *Western Union*, starring Richard Anderson; *Texas Gunfighter*, starring James Wilson; *Cavalry Patrol*, starring Dewey Martin; *Man From Denver*, starring James Whitmore; and *Simon Lash*, starring Jock Mahoney. And there were countless others, but despite the pilots that never left the gate, television ran many great classic Westerns.

THE MARSHAL OF TRAIL CITY

Starring "Wild" Bill Elliott

CAST:

"Wild" Bill Elliott	William Elliott
Cannonball	Dub Taylor

Westerns dominated television in the 1950s and 1960s, yet many pilot shows produced were never sold or made it past the screening room. It is uncertain how many workable Westerns were shelved and discarded in this period. The studios couldn't load their guns and cameras fast enough to shoot for another hit television Western. Movie legends were trying to make a transition from the big screen to television because the movie industry was slow. Many were not able to make the change because there simply was not enough airtime for more Westerns. Movie cowboys from the B Westerns were busy producing pilots, hoping to sell their guns to a new audience. Roy Rogers, Gene Autry, and William Boyd were among the few able to survive in television. Some of the unsold pilots produced between 1950 and 1960 were: *Western Union* in 1960 starring Richard Anderson, *Texas Gunfighter* in 1959 starring James Wilson, and *El Coyote Rides* in 1957 starring B-Western legend "Wild" Bill Elliott.

The Marshal of Trail City, filmed in 1950 by Century Television Productions, was another pilot starring "Wild" Bill Elliott which never developed into a series for reasons unknown. Elliott portrayed his movie-image "I'm a peaceable man" philosophy who becomes the marshal of Trail City, a town near his ranch. Trail City is the end of a long trail for Texas cattle herds

William Elliott

and a town made up of trail drivers, gunhands, and other restless souls who have never learned to respect any law except that of a blazing six-gun.

"Wild" Bill Elliott died November 26, 1965.

28

ARRAY OF TELEVISION WEAPONS

Shown here are some of television's most famous weapons. These were the guns the villains feared the most in every episode of a popular television Western.

These irons were prominent players in the show and the hero's best friend.*

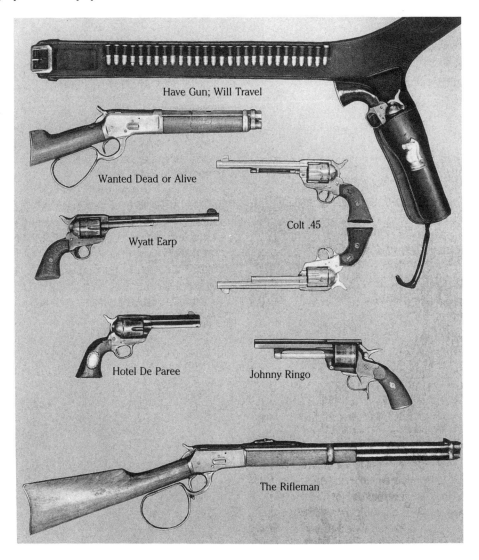

Have Gun; Will Travel

Wanted Dead or Alive

Wyatt Earp

Colt .45

Hotel De Paree

Johnny Ringo

The Rifleman

*Chuck Connors once thought he would make his name with a baseball bat, playing with the Brooklyn Dodgers and Chicago Cubs more than four decades ago.

But what made him famous was a rifle—an 1873 Winchester, with a big ring lever that Connors had custom made so he could twirl the rifle like a six-shooter.

That rifle, which became Connors' trademark from his TV show, *The Rifleman*, will be sold at auction with the rest of the actor's estate at C.B. Charles Galleries in Pompano Beach on the weekend of Feb. 12 and 13.

Connors, who died at age 71 in November 1992, actually used three of the rifles on the show, which ran for five seasons from 1958 to 1963 and still runs in syndication.

Gallery owner C.B. Charles said one of the rifles is owned by another famous cowboy actor, Gene Autry, who put it in his museum in California. *The Rifleman's* second Winchester was bought by former Nixon Cabinet member William Simon, Charles said.

Both of those men are worth millions, so they could afford to pay what people of lesser means would consider serious money for a collector's item. *The Rifleman's* third Winchester, which will be sold through sealed bid, will probably cost as much as a fairly expensive new car.

"We feel it should bring between $25,000 and $30,000," Charles said.

From *Sun-Sentinel*, January 1994

THE SHOWS

William Boyd and Topper

THE HOPALONG CASSIDY SHOW

Starring William Boyd

CREDITS:

NBC: June 24, 1949 through December 23, 1951 (99 episodes); Produced by: William Boyd Productions; Executive Producer: William Boyd; Producer: Toby Auguist.

CAST:

Hopalong Cassidy . . . . . . William Boyd
Red Connors . . . . Edgar Buchanan

The first significant Western to appear on network television was *The Hopalong Cassidy Show,* which began in 1949. It starred movie-cowboy legend William Boyd as Hopalong, a character he had played in sixty-six movies between 1935 and 1948.

Already a star for nearly twenty years, Boyd had accepted the role for the movies in the mid-thirties but was unhappy with how his character was portrayed and wanted changes made. In the original movie script, Hoppy was a ranch foreman, chewed tobacco, drank heavily, had a hard-nosed personality, and walked with a limp, thus earning himself the nickname Hopalong. By the time the second movie was written, he had cleaned up his act, and his limp had mysteriously disappeared.

In *The Hopalong Cassidy Show* on television, Hoppy was still owner of the Bar 20 Ranch and had a sidekick, Red Connors, who was the perfect foil for Cassidy, who, unlike most cowboy heroes, dressed all in black and, with his snow-white hair, cut quite a figure atop his horse Topper.

William Boyd died September 12, 1972.
Edgar Buchanan died April 4, 1979.

THE LONE RANGER

Starring Clayton Moore and
Jay Silverheels

CREDITS:

ABC: September 15, 1949 through September 4, 1965 (221 episodes); Produced by: The Wrather Corporation; Producers: George W. Trendle, Sherman Harris, Jack Chertok, Harry Poppe, Paul Landers; Directors: Paul Landers, Charles Livingston, John Morse, Earl Bellamy, George B. Seitz, Jr., Oscar Rudolph; Music: Ralph Cushman, Elias Alfriede; Theme: G. Rossini.

CAST:

The Lone Ranger . . . . . . Clayton Moore
The Lone Ranger
   (Fourth season) . . . . John Hart
Tonto . . . . Jay Silverheels

Perhaps the most famous television Western of all is *The Lone Ranger.* It was the tale of the mysterious masked man and his faithful Indian companion and their efforts to maintain law and order throughout the West. *The Lone Ranger* had begun as a local radio show in Detroit in 1933 and soon spread to a nationwide hookup. It came to TV in 1949 in a series of half-hour films epitomizing the good guys vs. the bad guys Western theme.

In the beginning, six Texas Rangers led by Capt. Dan Reid in search of a bunch of outlaws known as the Cavendish gang are ambushed at Bryant's Gap. All of the Rangers are shot and left for dead. A Mohawk Indian, Tonto, comes upon the massacre and discovers one Lone Ranger still alive. Tonto carries the seriously wounded man to a cave and nurses him back to health. John Reid, the surviving ranger, tells his story to Tonto, and later tears a piece of black material from his dead brother Dan Reid's vest and makes a mask which enabled him to hide his identity and to pose as an outlaw to get near the gang. Later, Reid and Tonto learn most of the outlaws had been hanged or imprisoned. To symbolize the massacre at Bryant's Gap, the Lone Ranger never removed his mask and continued to pursue outlaws and defend justice every week with his faithful Indian companion Tonto, his equally faithful steed Silver, and his legendary silver bullets, never fired in anger.

Jay Silverheels died March 5, 1980.

Clayton Moore and Jay Silverheels

Clayton Moore and Silver

THE MARSHAL OF GUNSIGHT PASS

Starring Russell Hayden

Russell Hayden

CREDITS:

ABC: March 12, 1950 through September 30, 1950 (22 episodes); Produced by: Gilford-Schlichter Productions; Producers: Philip Booth, Lou Holzer; Directors: Philip Booth, Frank Fox; Music performed by Andy Parker and the Plainsmen (a Western string band).

CAST:

Marshal (First)	Russell Hayden
Marshal (Second)	Eddie Dean
Marshal (Third)	Riley Hill
Deputy Roscoe	Roscoe Ates
Ruth	Jane Adrian

This low-budget half-hour Western of television's pioneering days, aimed at the kid audience, was based on the radio show of the same title. The television series, possibly the only Western action series produced live in a studio, had its share of cast problems. Its leading star as the marshal, Russell Hayden, was replaced by Eddie Dean, a well-known singing cowboy, after only four episodes. Four months later Dean handed over the marshal's badge to yet another hero, Riley Hill, who finished out the last few episodes. *The Marshal of Gunsight Pass* ran out of ammunition after just six months on the air.

This television Western was a story of a marshal who performed his duties in maintaining law and order in the small town of Gunsight Pass in the 1880s. The marshal was assisted by his deputy (Eddie Dean's longtime stuttering sidekick, Roscoe Ates) while facing the usual array of B-Western troubles: gunfights, bank robberies, cattle rustling, and no-good varmints. All these and more found their way into Gunsight Pass, but, on the other hand, with a name like Gunsight Pass, why wouldn't they?

Russell Hayden died June 10, 1981.

Roscoe Ates died March 1, 1962.

Eddie Dean and Roscoe Ates

George "Gabby" Hayes

THE GABBY HAYES SHOW

Starring Gabby Hayes

CREDITS:

NBC: December 11, 1950 through January 1, 1954 and ABC: May 12, 1956 through July 14, 1956; Produced by: NBC; Producer: Martin Stone, Joe Clair, E. Roger Muir; Director: Vincent J. Donehue.

CAST:

Gabby Hayes . . . . . George "Gabby" Hayes

The Gabby Hayes Show was a Western program geared to kids in 1950 with Gabby as the host. It ran for fifteen minutes on NBC just before *Howdy Doody*, and was expanded to a half hour after moving to ABC. Grizzled George "Gabby" Hayes was long the celebrated sidekick of such well known Western stars as John Wayne, Roy Rogers, and Gene Autry.

This show ran first on NBC and then on ABC late afternoons Monday through Friday for an audience of young "whippersnappers," as he would call them. Gabby spun yarns, showed scenes from the Western movies of the cowboy legends, and visited with the kids talking about their favorite Western heroes. Many of the clips were of B cowboys of the 1930s and 1940s, featuring Wayne, Tex Ritter, Sunset Carson, "Wild" Bill Elliott, William Boyd, and others. Gabby's distinctive voice, pepper beard, and cranky but homey and affectionate personality provided many enjoyable afternoons for his admiring fans.

George "Gabby" Hayes died February 9, 1969.

THE CISCO KID

Starring Duncan Renaldo and Leo Carrillo

CREDITS:

Syndicated: 1950–56 (156 episodes); Produced by: ZIV Television Productions; Producer: Walter Schwimmer; Director: Eddie Davis, Paul Landers, Lambert Hillyer, Leslie Goodwins, Sobey Martin; Music: Albert Glasser.

CAST:

Cisco Kid . . . . Duncan Renaldo
Pancho . . . . Leo Carrillo

The Cisco Kid was one of the first television Westerns in the early 1950s and became very popular with kids. This durable series was based on the character created by short-story writer O. Henry. Although the series was initially seen in black and white, all 156 episodes were filmed in color, which was long before color television became a home standard, and are rerun in color in syndication.

The Cisco Kid had a long history on the big screen with Warner Baxter playing the role initially in *In Old Arizona* (1928) and winning an Oscar. Baxter played

Duncan Renaldo
and Leo Carrillo

Leo Carrillo as Pancho

Duncan Renaldo and Leo Carrillo in a scene from *The Cisco Kid*

the happy-go-lucky bandit several more times in the thirties, before the role was taken over by Cesar Romero, then Gilbert Roland, and finally Duncan Renaldo, who played it many times before moving with it to television.

It was the story of the gallant Cisco Kid, and his often bumbling sidekick Pancho, who wore fancy clothes and fought the bad guys in New Mexico Territory. (Cisco originally was a sort of Old West Robin Hood in the O. Henry books.) This popular duo will be remembered for their humorous bantering. The gay caballeros could be seen every week righting wrongs, being insulted by the beautiful ladies they had just rescued, laughing it off, and then riding off into the sunset in another exciting tale of the Old West.

In late 1993, the Cisco Kid was dusted off for a new generation, with Jimmy Smits teaming with Cheech Marin (as Pancho).

Duncan Renaldo died September 3, 1980.

Leo Carrillo died September 10, 1961.

THE GENE AUTRY SHOW

Starring Gene Autry

CREDITS:

CBS: July 23, 1950 through August 7, 1956 (104 episodes); Produced by: Gene Autry's Flying A Produc-

Gene Autry and Champion

THE ROY ROGERS SHOW

Starring Roy Rogers

CREDITS:

NBC: December 30, 1951 through June 23, 1957 (104 episodes); Produced by: Roy Rogers Productions; Executive Producer: Roy Rogers; Producer: Jack Lacey, Bob Henry; Music: Lou Bring; Theme ("Happy Trails to You"): Dale Evans.

CAST:

Roy Rogers	Himself
Dale Evans	Herself
Pat Brady	Himself
Sheriff Potter	Harry Harvey, Sr.
and the Sons of the Pioneers	

Dale Evans, Trigger and Roy Rogers

Photo: Courtesy of Roy Rogers

tions; Executive Producers: Gene Autry, Armand Schaefer; Producer: Louis Gray; Directors: William Berke, Frank McDonald, Thomas Carr, George Archinbaud, Ray Nazarro, Ross Lederman.

CAST:

Gene Autry	Himself
Pat Buttram	Himself
Gail Davis	Herself

The Gene Autry Show debuted in 1950 and starred one of America's most popular singing cowboys. It was produced by his Flying A Productions and filmed on his famous Melody Ranch. Gene's hit record, "Back in the Saddle Again," became the theme song for his television series.

Playing himself in this Western as a roving defender of range justice, Gene often worked as an undercover marshal with his comic sidekick, Pat Buttram, who helped him keep on pitch while maintaining law and order in the Old West.

Gene Autry produced many other popular television Westerns: *The Range Rider*; *Buffalo Bill, Jr.*; *Annie Oakley*; and *The Adventures of Champion*.

43

Roy Rogers, Dale Evans, and sidekick, Pat Brady

The Roy Rogers Show was a popular contemporary Western in the early 1950s and geared mostly to kids. Roy Rogers was known as "King of the Cowboys" with his beautiful Palomino horse Trigger. The show featured Roy's wife and regular leading lady, Dale Evans, and sidekick Pat Brady, who rode around in his cantankerous jeep called "Nellybelle."

Roy and Dale lived on their Double R Bar Ranch located outside of Mineral City. Dale operated a diner in town with Pat Brady as the cook. Whenever trouble arrived and town Sheriff Potter needed help to enforce law and order, he beat a rapid path to Roy's doorstep. Roy, Dale, and Pat dropped what they were doing and took out after the varmints in their efforts to keep Mineral City crime-free.

Roy and Dale, along with Pat and the Sons of the Pioneers, later starred in a short-lived Western musical

Roy Rogers and Bullet take a break from chasing the bad guys in Mineral City.

variety series (1962) on ABC. It was titled *The Roy Rogers and Dale Evans Show*.

Pat Brady died February 27, 1972.

Trigger died at age 33 in 1965.

Kirby Grant as Sky King

SKY KING

Starring Kirby Grant

CREDITS:

NBC: September 16, 1951 through September 3, 1952; Produced by: Jack Chertok Productions; Executive Producer: Darrell McGowan; Producers: Clark Playlow, Jack Chertok; Directors: Jodie Copeland, William Witney, Stuart McGowan, Oliver Drake, Paul Landers; Music: Alec Compinsky.

CAST:

Sky King	Kirby Grant
Penny King	Gloria Winters
Clipper King	Ron Hagerthy
Sheriff Mitch	Ewing Mitchell

Sky King had its premiere in September of 1951 and ran weekly on NBC for a year, and then in reruns for years first on ABC, then on CBS. Originally it was a radio favorite dating back to 1947. This one had a new twist. The hero was a cowboy rancher who got around in his own plane rather than on horseback. Sky King was a pilot-rancher living with his niece and nephew, Penny and Clipper, on the Flying Crown Ranch located near Grover City, Arizona.

Whether Sky King was at the controls of his twin-engine Cessna, "The Songbird," or in the saddle, the criminals were in trouble. The sheriff of Grover City always called on Schuyler (Sky) King to help him chase them.

Sky King had a universal appeal to adult and children alike. His final program was shown in 1952, but the series has been revitalized between network and syndication and was seen as late as the 1980s, which seems to indicate the networks' desire to keep *Sky King* on the air.

Kirby Grant died in a car accident October 30, 1985, near Cape Canaveral, Florida, ironically on his way to the ill-fated liftoff of the Space Shuttle Challenger.

Lash LaRue

Legendary Western film star Lash LaRue hosted this fifteen-minute short-lived series in the early 1950s. LaRue was known as "King of the Bullwhip" in his popular B-Western movies of the forties.

In the opening of this show, Lash appeared in a modern-day marshal's office and began to talk about his grandfather Lash LaRue, the famous Western movie hero. This was somewhat confusing, simply because Lash was pretending to be the grandson who looked the spitting image of the cowboy star. He showed a selection of short clips from the movies and elaborated on how his grandfather captured the bad guys. Often his deputy, bewhiskered Fuzzy Q. Jones, was on hand to fill in some points. He was played by Al "Fuzzy" St. John, one of the veteran cowboy sidekicks in Westerns going back to the early days of sound. Sometimes Lash was seen talking to some old-timer about an action scene, which invariably thrilled his youthful audience.

Al "Fuzzy" St. John died January 21, 1963.

THE RANGE RIDER

Starring Jock Mahoney and Dick Jones

CREDITS:

Syndicated: 1951–54 (78 episodes); Produced by: Range Rider Productions, Gene Autry's Flying A Productions; Executive Producer: Armand Schaefer; Producer: Louis Gray, Hugh McCollum; Directors: Don McDougall, Thomas Carr, George Archinbaud, Frank McDonald; Music: Carl Cotner.

CAST:

The Range Rider . . . . Jock Mahoney
Dick West . . . . Dick Jones

Gene Autry and his Flying A Productions were responsible for this early television Western, *The Range Rider*. The theme song for the show was "Home on the Range," and no one could be more at home on the range to play the starring role than Jock Mahoney, a six foot four inch actor-stuntman. Also starring in the series was another actor-stuntman, Dick Jones, as his sidekick Dick West. There were 76 *Range Rider* episodes filmed, and then Dick Jones went on to star in another television Western, *Buffalo Bill, Jr.,* which was

LASH OF THE WEST

Starring Lash LaRue

CREDITS:

ABC: January 4, 1953 through April 26, 1953; Produced by: Screen Guild Productions; Producer: Lash LaRue.

CAST:

Host . . . . Al "Lash" LaRue
Fuzzy Q. Jones . . . . Al "Fuzzy" St. John
Old-timer . . . . Flapjack

produced by Gene Autry. Jock Mahoney would later star in CBS's *Yancy Derringer*.

Viewers thrilled to the exciting tales of the West about a nameless man who called himself the Range Rider and his young sidekick Dick West, as they rode through the badlands defending justice. The scenes were original and loaded with action as both the Range Rider and Dick West chased the bad guys in the lawless years of California during the 1860s. In each episode, there always seemed to be a beautiful lady who caught the Range Rider's attention. In true cowboy fashion, he tipped his hat, then rode off into the sunset in pursuit of another adventure.

Jock Mahoney died December 14, 1989.

Jock Mahoney (left) and Dick Jones

Jock Mahoney as *The Range Rider*

WILD BILL HICKOK

Starring Guy Madison and Andy Devine

CREDITS:

Syndicated: 1951–56 (113 episodes); Produced by: Screen Gems; Executive Producer: William F. Broidy; Producer: Wesley Barry; Director: Jean Yarbrough.

CAST:

Wild Bill Hickok . . . . Guy Madison
Jingles P. Jones . . . . Andy Devine

Wild Bill Hickok was one of television's most popular standbys in the early 1950s. It was filled with action and humor. And it had matinee idol Guy Madison in the title role.

It featured the exploits of James Butler (Wild Bill) Hickok, a United States Marshal who traveled with his

Guy Madison

Andy Devine as Jingles

Guy Madison and Andy Devine

49

jovial sidekick Jingles, and described their attempts battling injustice in lawless territories during the 1870s.

Wild Bill Hickok was a favorite among kids as well as adults, and if you close your eyes and listen hard, you can still hear Jingles yelling, "Hey, Wild Bill, wait for me!"

The series originally began in syndication, but later was picked up first by CBS and then by ABC. There also was a concurrent but different radio version in the early fifties starring Guy Madison and Andy Devine.

Andy Devine died February 18, 1977.

DEATH VALLEY DAYS

Host Stanley Andrews

CREDITS:

Syndicated: 1952–75 (532 episodes); Produced by: Madison Productions for 20 Mule Team Borax Company; Producer: Darrell McGowan; Director: Stuart McGowan.

HOST:

The Old Ranger (1952–65) . .	Stanley Andrews
Host (1965–66)	Ronald Reagan
Host (1966–69)	Robert Taylor
Host (1969–72)	Dale Robertson

Dating back to radio days in the 1930s and initially created by a woman, *Death Valley Days* was a thirty-minute television Western anthology series depicting true stories of many famous and infamous characters from the Old West, who lived or traveled through Death Valley. Among them were Wild Bill Hickok and the notorious outlaw Belle Starr. *Death Valley Days,* one of the most durable of all television Westerns, opened each week with an introductory scene showing a twenty-mule team pulling a train of wagons hauling borax, a mineral discovered in Death Valley and used in ceramics and in working with gold. Following this, the Old Ranger (Stanley Andrews, host of the show) brought a new tale from the many lifestyles of the

Stanley Andrews as The Old Ranger

Ronald Reagan in *Death Valley Days*

Gail Davis

Western Frontier. The Old Ranger was host of the show from 1952 until his death in 1965, when he was replaced by various movie and television stars, including Ronald Reagan (who then left for politics), Robert Taylor, Dale Robertson, Rory Calhoun, and Merle Haggard.

Approximately two dozen new episodes were produced every year, several filmed on location in Death Valley.

ANNIE OAKLEY

Starring Gail Davis

CREDITS:

Syndicated: April 1953 through December 1956 (81 episodes); Produced by: Gene Autry's Flying A Productions; Executive Producer: Armand Schaefer; Producers: Colbert Clark, Louis Gray; Directors: Don McDougall, Frank McDonald, Thomas Carr, George

Archinbaud, Ross Lederman, William Berke; Music: Erma Levin; Theme: Ben Weisman, Fred Wise; Theme Song Performer: Gail Davis.

CAST:

Annie Oakley	Gail Davis
Deputy Sheriff Lofty Craig	Brad Johnson
Tagg Oakley	Jimmy Hawkins

Annie Oakley was a popular television Western series in the early 1950s based loosely on the life of the real historical figure (1859–1926). *Annie Oakley*, a sharpshooter of the Wild West, was television's first female heroine. Gail Davis, the star, was a Gene Autry discovery and had been featured in a number of his films and television Westerns.

In this pigtails-and-pistols Western, Annie and her younger brother Tagg were invited to live with Deputy Sheriff Lofty Craig after the death of their parents, and he became her silent suitor. Annie emerged an expert with a six-shooter and was an adept rider as well, using her expertise as a markswoman to help Craig uphold law and order in Diablo County, Arizona, during the 1860s, just "doin' what came naturally."

Gail Davis as *Annie Oakley*

Interestingly, a young Fess Parker was a semiregular on the show as Tom Courier, editor of the *Diablo Courier*.

THE ADVENTURES OF RIN TIN TIN

Starring Lee Aaker

CREDITS:

ABC: October 15, 1954 through September 29, 1957 (164 episodes); Produced by: Screen Gems; Executive Producer: Herbert B. Leonard; Producer: Fred Briskin; Directors: Robert Walker, Fred Vickman, Earl Bellamy, Lew Sanders, Douglas Heyes; Music: Hal Hopper.

CAST:

Corporal Rusty	Lee Aaker
Lt. Ripley "Rip" Masters	James L. Brown
Corporal Randy Boone	Rand Brooks
Sgt. Aloysius "Biff" O'Hara	Joe Sawyer

The Adventures of Rin Tin Tin showcased one of television's earliest canine heroes who left big paw prints for his descendants to follow. Rin Tin Tin was the only dog in Los Angeles to be listed in the telephone directory. Lee Duncan, his owner and trainer, said, "Rinty was very close to his great grandfather," the original Rin Tin Tin, who appeared in many popular motion pictures of the 1930s and the 1940s, and was for a time the highest paid performer (actor?) in films. The first Rin Tin Tin was found by Duncan as a five-day-old puppy in an abandoned German dugout in the Chateau Thierry section of France in 1918.

The first episode of this canine crime fighter series commenced when the U.S. Cavalry came upon a wagon train that had been attacked by Apache Indians. The only survivors were a young boy named Rusty and his German shepherd he called Rin Tin Tin. The cavalry took the boy and his dog to Fort Apache in Arizona, where Lt. Ripley "Rip" Masters made Rusty a corporal so he could stay on at the fort.

In one episode of *Rin Tin Tin*, Corporal Rusty and Rinty discovered a conspiracy to assassinate a gen-

James Brown
Lee Aaker, and Rinty

54

James L. Brown, Rinty and Lee Aaker

eral, and the boy reported the information to Rip, preventing the tragedy. Rusty and Rin Tin Tin performed their weekly duties taking a bite out of crime in 164 episodes.

DAVY CROCKETT

Starring Fess Parker

CREDITS:

ABC: December 15, 1954 through December 14, 1955 (a five-part chronicle over a twelve-month period); Produced by: Walt Disney Productions; Producer: Bill Walsh; Director: Norman Foster; Music: George Bruns; Theme: George Bruns, Tom Blackburn.

CAST:

Davy Crockett	Fess Parker
George Russell	Buddy Ebsen
Polly Crockett	Helen Stanley

Billy Crockett	Eugene Brindle
Johnny Crockett	Ray Whiteside
Thimbelrig	Hans Conried
Mike Fink	Jeff York
Jim Bowie	Kenneth Tobey
Big Foot Mason	Mike Mazurki

One of television's most successful Westerns was the classic *Davy Crockett*, a five-part series broadcast in segments on Walt Disney's *Frontierland* and *Disneyland*. The first three, covering the period up to his death at the siege of the Alamo, were then packaged into a hugely successful feature film, followed by another feature packaged from the remaining two episodes. This Western single-handedly launched Disney in television and was responsible for other great Westerns: *Zorro*, *Texas John Slaughter*, *Elfego Baca*, and others.

It followed the fictional adventures of Davy Crockett, a legendary frontiersman, who became one of American history's most famous heroes during the 1800s. Davy Crockett was known as "King of the Wild Frontier," a noble warrior and Indian fighter. His last days, of course, were at the Alamo, where he died with

Fess Parker

Fess Parker as *Davy Crockett*

another hero Jim Bowie. Their attempts to survive the attack of a Mexican army of nearly two hundred renegades had been unsuccessful.

In the early 1990s, Fess Parker, long retired, was coaxed into stepping back into the role of Crockett, reminiscing about his early adventures, for a new Disney series which was short-lived. He declined, and Johnny Cash took the part.

STORIES OF THE CENTURY

Starring Jim Davis

CREDITS:

Syndicated: 1954–56 (39 episodes); Produced by: Republic Pictures; Producer: Rudy Ralston; Director: Joe Kane; Music: Gerald Roberts; Narrator: Marvin Miller.

CAST:

Matt Clark	Jim Davis
Frankie Adams	Mary Castle
Margaret "Jonesy" Jones (later)	Kristine Miller

Stories of the Century, a spin-off of a pilot called *Last Stagecoach West*, was based on official records from

Jim Davis in a scene from
Stories of the Century

the newspaper files of that era. Each episode of this Western was filled with action from history's most infamous outlaws, like Belle Starr, the Younger brothers, the Daltons, Billy the Kid, and Frank and Jesse James. B-Western cowboy Jim Davis starred before later playing Jock Ewing in the hit show *Dallas*. Mary Castle, who initially played his partner Frankie Adams, left her role in *Stories of the Century* and was replaced by Kristine Miller as "Jonesy" Jones.

The series followed stalwart Matt Clark, an investigator for the Southwestern Railroad Company, who did his best to protect its passengers and shipments against holdups, Indian attacks, and vicious outlaws during the 1890s. Matt's female partner assisted him in the investigation of any trouble that plagued the railroad and, working undercover, would normally arrive in town alone ahead of him to scout out information about the outlaws. She would supply Matt with all the details about the suspects they were tracking, and then they would move in on the bad guys.

Although a syndicated show, *Stories of the Century* won an Emmy as Best Western or Adventure Series of 1954.

THE LIFE AND LEGEND OF WYATT EARP

Starring Hugh O'Brian

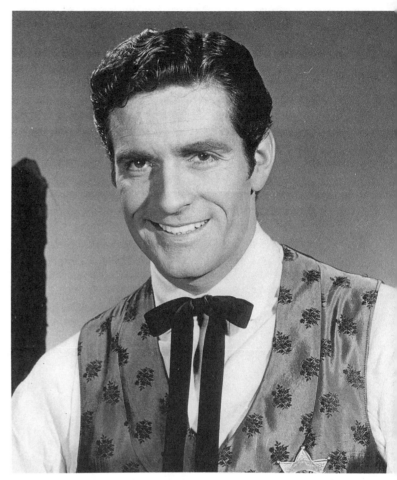

Hugh O'Brian

CREDITS:

ABC: September 6, 1955 through September 26, 1961 (266 episodes); Produced by: Wyatt Earp Enterprises, Desilu Productions; Executive Producers: Robert Sisk, Louis F. Edelman; Producer: Roy Rowland; Director: Frank McDonald; Theme: Harry Adamson, Harry Warren; Theme Song Performers: Ken Darby Singers.

CAST:

Marshal Wyatt Earp	Hugh O'Brian
Deputy Morgan Earp	Dirk London
Deputy Virgil Earp	John Anderson
Shotgun Gibbs	Morgan Woodward
Doc Holliday	Myron Healey
Ned Buntline	Lloyd Corrigan
Sheriff John Behan	Lash LaRue
Old Man Clanton	Trevor Bardette
Bat Masterson	Alan Dinehart

The Life and Legend of Wyatt Earp was loosely based on the protagonist's life story and dealt with mature subjects and actual heroes of the West. Perhaps one of the first adult Westerns, it was still a favorite among youthful viewers.

The series told of Wyatt Earp, a former lawman of Dodge City, Kansas, who had become U.S. Marshal of Tombstone, Arizona, after his predecessor was gunned down. Earp had a reputation as a tough lawman which meant respect but could also spell trouble.

Of special interest in this show was Earp's gun, designed by famed showman and biographer Ned Buntline, called the Buntline Special. The gun had a foot-long barrel and was as accurate as a rifle. Wyatt could draw and hit his opponent at a greater distance than with the normal standard weapon. Some episodes of interest were those pertaining to Wyatt's long battle with the Clanton gang who more or less ran the town before he arrived. Then, of course, came the famous shoot-out at the O.K. Corral, a gunfight never to be forgotten in the minds and hearts of all Wild West enthusiasts. This showdown came in the five-part finale to the series.

Dick Jones

Hugh O'Brian in *The Life and Legend of Wyatt Earp*

BUFFALO BILL, JR.

Starring Dick Jones

CREDITS:

Syndicated: 1955 (52 episodes); Produced by: Gene Autry's Flying A Productions; Executive producer: Armand Schaefer; Producers: Gene Autry, Eric Jenson, Lois Gray; Director: John English, George Archinbaud,

Don McDougall, Frank McDonald, Robert Walker, Thomas Carr, William McCarthy; Music: Carl Cotner.

CAST:

Buffalo Bill, Jr.	Dick Jones
Calamity	Nancy Gilbert
Judge Ben Wiley	Harry Cheshire

Buffalo Bill, Jr., a popular television Western during the 1950s, was produced by Gene Autry. Dick Jones, the show's star, had previously been Jock Mahoney's sidekick in *The Range Rider,* another Autry Western, and performed his own stunts in both series, which were filmed on Autry's Melody Ranch movie location.

It was the story of Buffalo Bill, Jr., and his young sister Calamity, orphans adopted by Judge Ben "Fair 'n' Square" Wiley after their parents were killed. Buffalo Bill, Jr., became the marshal of Wileyville, Texas, aided by Calamity, defending the law during the 1890s. Judge Wiley, founder of Wileyville, was the magistrate of this small Texas town and helped young Bill protect its citizens. Gene Autry led us to believe that Buffalo Bill, Jr. was the son of William F. Cody, frontier scout turned showman. However, it was probably fiction.

JUDGE ROY BEAN

Starring Edgar Buchanan

CREDITS:

Syndicated: 1955–57 (39 episodes); Produced by: Quintet Productions; Producer: Russell Hayden; Director: Reg Browne.

CAST:

Judge Roy Bean	Edgar Buchanan
Jeff Taggard	Jack Buetel
Letty Bean	Jackie Loughery
Steve	Russell Hayden

Judge Roy Bean featured the exploits of a real-life smalltown storekeeper who appointed himself judge of Langtry, Texas, a town named for famed nineteenth-century actress Lillie Langtry, on whom it has been said Bean had an undying crush. Bean was to proclaim himself "the law west of the Pecos."

During the 1870s the wildest spot in the United States was the lawless region west of the Pecos River, on the frontier beyond the reach of the authorities. The railroads, then pushing their way West, attracted the most vicious characters in the expanding nation. It was said that all civilization and law stopped at the east banks of the Pecos. One lone storekeeper took it upon himself to change all this, fairly or unfairly; his name was Judge Roy Bean.

(Bean was played most memorably on the big screen by Walter Brennan in *The Westerner* and by Paul Newman in *The Life and Times of Judge Roy Bean.*)

Edgar Buchanan died April 14, 1979.

Jack Buetel died June 27, 1989.

Edgar Buchanan as Judge Roy Bean

Fury

FURY

Starring Peter Graves and
Bobby Diamond

CREDITS:

NBC: September 15, 1955 through September 3, 1960 (114 episodes); Produced by: Independent Television Corporation (ITC); Executive Producer: Leon Fromkess; Producers: Leon Fromkess, Irving Cummings, Ray Nazarro; Director: Ray Nazarro.

CAST:

Jim Newton	Peter Graves
Joey Newton	Bobby Diamond
Pete	William Fawcett
Packey Lambert	Roger Mobley
Pee Wee Jenkins	Jimmy Baird
Helen Watkins	Ann Robinson
Harriet Newton	Nan Leslie

William Fawcett, Peter Graves, and Bobby Diamond

GUNSMOKE

Starring James Arness

CREDITS:

CBS: September 10, 1955 through September 1, 1975 (233 thirty-minute episodes and 400 sixty-minute episodes); Produced by: Arness Productions; Executive Producers: John Mantley, Charles Marquis Warren, Philip Leacock; Producers: Norman MacDonnell, Jo-

Peter Graves as Jim Newton

James Arness

Fury was another modern-day Western for children debuting in the mid-1950s. It was similar to other contemporary shows such as *Lassie* and *My Friend Flicka* and revolved around a horse and the boy who loved him.

In the first episode, Jim Newton, a widower who owned the Broken Wheel Ranch located outside of Capitol City, went into town to get supplies. A local orphan, Joey, was playing baseball with a group of other boys when one accidentally broke a window. Joey was blamed, but Jim, who happened to witness the incident, cleared his name, became close to him and adopted Joey into his family, presenting Joey with a beautiful black stallion which he named Fury.

Fury was a hero many times, preventing harm coming to family members in distress or helping capture criminals trespassing on the Newton property. There was no question who the hero was in this series nor his preference for oats, but it also was the story of an orphan's growth toward manhood. Fury was owned and trained by Ralph McCutcheon.

Fury was known in syndication as *Brave Stallion*.

James Arness as Matt Dillon

James Arness and
Dennis Weaver in
Gunsmoke

seph Drackow, Leonard Katzman; Directors: Charles
Marquis Warren, Victor French, Robert Butler, Ted
Post, Andrew V. McLaglen, Vincent McEveety, Bernard
McEveety, Mark Rydell, Christian I. Nyby II; Music:
Jerrold Immel, Rex Koury, John Parker, Richard
Shores.

CAST:

Marshal Matt Dillon	James Arness
Kitty Russell	Amanda Blake
Doc Galen Adams	Milburn Stone
Chester Goode	Dennis Weaver
Festus Hagen	Ken Curtis
Newly O'Brien	Buck Taylor
Sam	Glenn Strange
Quint Asper	Burt Reynolds
Thad Greenwood	Roger Ewing

On September 10, 1955, John Wayne introduced *Gunsmoke* on CBS, which would become the longest

Ken Curtis as Deputy Marshal Festus Hagen

James Arness, Milburn Stone, Amanda Blake, Ken Curtis, and Burt Reynolds

Milburn Stone as Doc Galen Adams

up again in 1987 for the first of several two-hour "return" movies over the next five years.

Milburn Stone died June 12, 1980.
Amanda Blake died August 16, 1989.
Glenn Strange died September 25, 1973.
Ken Curtis died April 28, 1991.

BRAVE EAGLE

Starring Keith Larsen

CREDITS:

CBS: September 28, 1955 through June 6, 1956; Produced by: Roy Rogers Productions; Executive Producers: Arthur Rush, Mike North; Producer: Jack Lacey.

running Western in television history. The landmark series, long a staple on radio, ran uninterrupted for twenty years on the network, and was the first Western of its kind that dealt with plots and scripts for an adult audience.

When *Gunsmoke* was being prepared for television, the lead role of Matt Dillon was offered to John Wayne, who turned it down because of his movie contracts but recommended a young friend and protegé, a lanky six-foot-six actor, James Arness, for the part. Needless to say, the network accepted his choice, and Arness took *Gunsmoke* to the number-one spot in the Nielsen ratings. The show was seldom out of the top ten.

Gunsmoke was the story of the fearless Matt Dillon, marshal of Dodge City, Kansas, during the 1880s. Violence was a commonplace infestation of notorious outlaws, gunslingers and cattle rustlers. Marshal Dillon and his gimpy deputy Chester Goode (and later, Festus Hagen) attempted to maintain law and order in Dodge City. Matt Dillon's romantic interest was Kitty Russell, owner of the Long Branch Saloon. Miss Kitty was a tough and strong-willed lady who always looked after the Marshal with more than just a proprietory eye. And then there was Doc Galen Adams, who could be counted on to patch a wound or deliver a baby in this remarkable Western favorite.

After twenty seasons on the network, Matt Dillon packed it in and headed for retirement, only to saddle

Keith Larsen

CAST:

Brave Eagle	Keith Larsen
Keena	Keena Nomleena
Morning Star	Kim Winona
Smokey Joe	Bert Wheeler
Black Cloud	Pat Hogan

Brave Eagle was a landmark but a forgotten television Western portraying the Indian as the good guy yet not relegating the white man as his enemy.

Brave Eagle presented a point of view through the eyes of the American Indian trying to survive in the untamed West of the early settlement days. A young Cheyenne chief gathered up his warriors many times and headed out to defend their ancient land. He never gave up hope that one day the Indians and the white man would live in peace. Brave Eagle struggled to teach his young adopted son Keena about charity and justice regardless of injustice being done to the Indian. Brave Eagle's romantic interest was the beautiful young maiden Morning Star, a full-blooded Sioux.

This show stands beside *Broken Arrow* and very few others in treating the Indian with respect and featuring one as the star of the series.

TALES OF THE TEXAS RANGERS

Starring Willard Parker and Harry Lauter

CREDITS:

CBS: September 3, 1955 through May 25, 1957 (52 episodes) later rerun on ABC; Produced by: Screen Gems; Executive Producer: Harry Briskin; Producers: Colbert Clark, Harry Ackerman, John Seinfield; Director: Lew Landers.

CAST:

Jace Pearson	Willard Parker
Clay Morgan	Harry Lauter

Tales of the Texas Rangers had as its source the files of America's oldest law enforcement organization. What

Willard Parker
and Harry Lauter

made this series different was the switching of each week's episode from modern-day situations with automobiles to stories of the Old West and wagons in the 1880s.

Whether galloping after a horse thief or chasing a car thief, Jace Pearson and Clay Morgan were devoted Texas Rangers who would not abandon the hunt until they captured their quarry. Using crime-detection methods appropriate to each era, they made certain that "a felon's lot was not a happy one."

Joel McCrea played Ranger Jace Pearson in the radio version of the show in the early 1950s.

Harry Lauter died October 30, 1990.

CHEYENNE

Starring Clint Walker

CREDITS:

ABC: September 13, 1955 through August 30, 1963 (107 episodes); Produced by: Warner Brothers Television; Executive Producer: William T. Orr; Producers: Arthur Silver, Roy Huggins, Harry Foster; Directors: Herbert L. Strock, William Hale, Lee Sholem, Douglas Heyes, Lew Landers, Richard L. Bare, Arthur Lubin; Music: William Lava, Stan Jones, Paul Sawtell; Theme: William Lava, Stan Jones.

CAST:

Cheyenne Bodie . . . . Clint Walker

One of the most popular Westerns in television history was *Cheyenne*. The character looked the way a rugged frontiersman should–six-foot-six, handsome, broad-shouldered, and equally broad-chested. This was the story of Cheyenne Bodie, a loner who roamed the Western Frontier in the 1870s fighting trouble, a white man who learned the Indian lifestyle as a young boy being raised by the Cheyenne tribe. Bodie was gentle and considerate and had the highest respect for the law; that is, if the law wasn't crooked, as he found in some towns. He often risked his life to help a weakly homesteader or rancher in distress who was defenseless against the bad guy. Bodie first would speak with his serious big voice, but if they didn't listen, he spoke with his Colt single-action army revolver.

In 1958, Clint Walker, the star of *Cheyenne*, walked out on the show in a dispute with the studio and was

Clint Walker as Cheyenne Bodie

Clint Walker in *Cheyenne*

Logo for *Cheyenne*

Clint Walker as Cheyenne Bodie

Clint Walker in a scene from an episode of *Cheyenne*

replaced by Ty Hardin as Bronco Layne. However, Walker and the studio ultimately settled their dispute and he returned to his famous role. *Bronco* then became a spin-off series on its own.

Cheyenne holds the distinction of being one of the first great Western series—it premiered three nights after *Gunsmoke*. Initially it was part of Warner's maiden series, *Warner Brothers Presents*, rotating with *Casablanca* and *Kings Row*. Those two movie spin-offs were quickly dropped, and *Cheyenne* stayed on.

Scene from *Cheyenne*

DICK POWELL'S ZANE GREY THEATRE

Starring Dick Powell

CREDITS:

CBS: October 5, 1956 through September 20, 1962 (145 episodes); Produced by: Four Star Productions; Producers: Aaron Spelling, Hal Hudson, Steven Lord; Directors: John English, Budd Boetticher, David Lowell Rich, Christian I. Nyby, Felix Feist; Music: Herschel Burke Gilbert, Joseph Mullendore.

CAST:

Host . . . . Dick Powell

Dick Powell's Zane Grey Theatre ran for six years on CBS. It was a Western anthology series similar to *Death Valley Days* and was hosted by the movie star Dick Powell. The stories were adapted basically from the novels of the author Zane Grey and featured top name stars such as Barbara Stanwyck, David Niven, Joseph Cotten, Edward G. Robinson, Walter Pidgeon, Jack

Dick Powell

Lemmon, Van Johnson, Hedy Lamarr, and Ida Lupino. Sometimes Powell himself would appear in the leading role. As one of the principals in the successful Four Star Productions, Dick Powell had full control over the casting of the show, which perhaps was the reason why he agreed to do the popular television series.

Dick Powell died January 2, 1963.

THE ADVENTURES OF JIM BOWIE

Starring Scott Forbes

CREDITS:

ABC: September 7, 1956 through August 29, 1958 (78 episodes); Produced by: Desilu Productions; Executive Producer: Louis F. Edelman; Producers: William H. Wright, Lewis Foster; Director: Hollingsworth Morse; Theme: Ken Darby.

CAST:

Jim Bowie	Scott Forbes
Rexin Bowie	Peter Hanson
Maw Bowie	Minerva Urecal
John James Audubon	Robert Cornthwaite

The Adventures of Jim Bowie was about a legendary hero who wore a knife on his hip instead of a six-gun. The setting was Louisiana Territory during the 1830s with its French-American New Orleans background.

Jim Bowie was a wealthy young adventurer and the inventor of a knife that bore his name. After being attacked by a grizzly bear when the blade of his knife broke in half, almost costing him his life, Bowie designed one with a stronger blade more suitable for the vigorous demands of frontier life. It would become

Scott Forbes
as Jim Bowie

known throughout the West as the famous Bowie knife.

Bowie's character in the series met up with such historical figures as Andrew Jackson, Sam Houston, Johnny Appleseed, and John James Audubon. Historically, in 1836, Jim Bowie and another hero, Davy Crockett, met their fate at the Alamo in Texas after a Mexican attack, but this was never shown in the series.

BROKEN ARROW

Starring John Lupton and
Michael Ansara

CREDITS:

ABC: September 25, 1956 through September 18, 1960 (73 episodes); Produced by: 20th Century-Fox Television; Producer: Mel Epstein; Directors: Bernard L. Kowalski, Alvin Ganzer, Charles Haas, Sam Peckinpah, Joseph Kane, Hollingsworth Morse; Music: Stanley Wilson, Paul Sawtell; Theme: Paul Sawtell, Ned Washington; Narrator: John Lupton.

CAST:

Tom Jeffords . . . . John Lupton
Chief Cochise . . . . Michael Ansara

Broken Arrow was a very successful television Western during the fifties based on the bestselling novel by Elliott Arnold and the hit 1950 movie which starred James Stewart and Jeff Chandler.

It followed the exploits of Tom Jeffords, an Indian agent to the Apaches in Tucson, and his relationship with Cochise, their chief. An encroachment by the white man, referred to by the Apaches as "White Eyes," led to many attacks on the Pony Express riders, preventing them from taking the mail across Apache land. Jeffords, fed up with the bloodbaths between the white man and the Apaches, risked his life riding alone to meet face to face with Cochise, gaining the latter's respect and trust by his bravery. Cochise agreed to a peace treaty, and Jeffords received the Broken Arrow, the Indian symbol for peace, friendship, and under-

Michael Ansara
and John Lupton

Michael Ansara as Cochise

Bill Williams as Kit Carson

76

standing, and their relationship grew to the point of becoming blood brothers. Together over the weeks they fought renegades, race prejudice, political corruption, and the plight of the American Indian.

In the original pilot, which aired in June 1956, Ricardo Montalban had the role of Cochise.

THE ADVENTURES OF KIT CARSON

Starring Bill Williams

CREDITS:

Syndicated: 1951–55 (104 episodes): Produced by: Revue Productions; Producer: Richard Irving; Director: Norman Lloyd.

CAST:

Christopher "Kit" Carson	Bill Williams
El Toro	Don Diamond

The Adventures of Kit Carson proved a popular Western in the early 1950s, geared for the children's market, although there was very little historical fact in this series about the real Kit Carson, famous Indian Scout and explorer of the Western Frontier.

Kit Carson and El Toro, his Mexican sidekick, roamed the Wild West, traveling from Wyoming to Texas during the 1880s, chasing desperadoes, tracking wild game, drinking coffee by their campfire, and delighting youthful audiences. This, of course, was historically inaccurate, since the real Kit Carson died in 1868 at age fifty-nine. At the time he was an Indian agent at Fort Lyon, Colorado.

Bill Williams died October 9, 1992.

RED RYDER

Starring Allan "Rocky" Lane

CREDITS:

Syndicated: 1956–57 (39 episodes); Produced by: Hollywood Television Service, Republic Pictures; Executive Producer: Allan "Rocky" Lane.

Allan "Rocky" Lane in *Red Ryder*

CAST:

Red Ryder	Allan "Rocky" Lane
Little Beaver	Louis Letteri
The Dutchess of Carson City . .	Elizabeth Slifer

Red Ryder was a familiar title among many Western movies. Several legendary movie cowboys portrayed this character, but the most famous was Allan "Rocky" Lane. When the B-Westerns had run their course on the big screen, Lane, like many other cowboys, decided to do his movie role in a television series.

This Western series dealt with the adventures of Red Ryder, who helped tame the lawless West with his diminutive sidekick, an Indian boy named Little Beaver, during the 1870s. Red Ryder attempted to maintain law and order with a little help from his little friend.

Although the series never interested the networks, it did survive thirty-nine episodes in syndication. "Rocky" Lane guest starred in many television Westerns over the years, but his most memorable contribution to television history was as the voice of Mr. Ed, the talking horse.

Allan "Rocky" Lane died October 24, 1973.

Tod Andrews as Major John Singleton Mosby

THE GRAY GHOST

Starring Tod Andrews

CREDITS:

Syndicated: 1957 (39 episodes); Produced by Lindsley Parsons Productions; Exectuive Producer: Lindsley Parsons.

CAST:

Maj. John Singleton Mosby . . .	Tod Andrews
Lieutenant St. Clair	Phil Cambridge

An unusual thirty-minute television Western with an unusual title, *The Gray Ghost* was quite underrated during its run in the 1950s. This forgotten series dealt with interesting stories about the Civil War and its cavalrymen, and was based on the true exploits of John Singleton Mosby, a Southern lawyer who initially supported the Union but changed his mind when the South seceded. He then joined the 43rd Battalion of the 1st Virginia Cavalry and organized an effective guerrilla unit.

When the Union Army became desperate in making an attempt to send troops into Confederate field territory, it recruited a woman spy, a double agent who exposed their plans to Mosby, a Confederate major. Later the Union Army learned of the woman's betrayal and sentenced her to death. Discovering that her identity had been uncovered, Mosby set up a dramatic raid attack on the Union camp and rescued her. Following this Confederate victory, the Union Army proclaimed Major Mosby their enemy and referred to him as the Gray Ghost.

There were many daring raids led by Major Mosby and the Confederates against the Union Army during the thirty-nine episodes filmed of *The Gray Ghost*.

THE RESTLESS GUN

Starring John Payne

CREDITS:

NBC: September 23, 1957 through September 14, 1959; (Rerun on ABC: October 12, 1959 through September 20, 1960) (77 episodes); Produced by: Window Glen Productions, Revue Productions; Executive Producer: John Payne; Producer: David Dortort; Music: Stanley Wilson; Theme: Michael Green, Michael Lenard, David Kahn; Narrator: John Payne.

CAST:

Vint Bonner . . . . John Payne

The Restless Gun featured motion picture star John Payne in his only television series. Payne was execu-

John Payne

tive producer and narrator of the show as well, which originated as a segment of *Schlitz Playhouse of Stars*, a CBS series.

The theme song, "I Ride With the Wind", explained the lifestyle of Vint Bonner, a Civil War veteran who wandered the West, drifting from town to town. Vint Bonner had a fearsome reputation as the fastest gunslinger during the postwar era but actually loathed violence. After the word spread about the speed of his Colt .45, Bonner rarely had a peaceful hour. It was either slap leather or push up daisies as each new gunslinger tried to beat him to the draw. On more than one occasion Bonner tried using reason instead of bullets. "Look," he said, "we're both too old for this kind of foolishness, especially on such a nice summer day." If the opponent agreed, he lived; if he found reason to make a disparaging remark, it was about the last words he ever uttered.

John Payne died December 6, 1989.

CASEY JONES

Starring Alan Hale

CREDITS:

Syndicated: 1957–59 (32 episodes); Produced by: Screen Gems; Producer: Harold Greene; Director: Lew Landers.

CAST:

Casey Jones	Alan Hale
Alice Jones	Mary Lawrence
Casey, Jr.	Bobby Clark
Redrock	Eddy Waller
Willie Simms	Dub Taylor
Sam Peachpit	Pat Hogan

Casey Jones was a Western adventure series based on the stories of the legendary railroad engineer of American folklore. The setting was Jackson, Tennessee, during the late 1890s. John Luther "Casey" Jones worked for the Illinois Central Railroad Company, which owned the famous steam engine locomotive called the Cannonball Express #1.

Casey Jones and his loyal crew aboard the Cannonball, including his fireman Willie Simms, had many encounters with the Indians and bad men along the route trying to keep the #1 running on schedule.

The real Casey Jones was killed when the train wrecked in Vaughan, Mississippi, on April 30, 1900. But the *Casey Jones* television series lives on in syndication. Its star, of course, went on to play the Skipper on *Gilligan's Island*.

Alan Hale died January 2, 1990.

Alan Hale Jr.

Tris Coffin
as Capt. Tom Rynning

TWENTY-SIX MEN

Starring Tris Coffin

CREDITS:

Syndicated: 1957–59 (78 episodes); Produced by: Russell Hayden; Executive Producer: Russell Hayden; Producer: James Baiser, William Dennis; Music: Hal Hopper, Gordon Zahler; Theme: Hal Hopper, Russell Hayden.

CAST:

Capt. Tom Rynning	Tris Coffin
Ranger Clint Travis	Kelo Henderson

Twenty-Six Men was based on true official files of the Arizona Rangers in the final days taming the Old West.

In 1901, a law enforcement organization was formed, known as the Arizona Rangers, consisting of twenty-six men: a captain, a lieutenant, four sergeants, and twenty privates. The Rangers preserved and maintained law and order in the Arizona Territory, making arrests of criminals in any part of Arizona.

As one of the original members reportedly recalled: "The reason there was only twenty-six of us was because the Territory couldn't afford no more."

Captain Tom Rynning and the Rangers were required to furnish their own guns, horses, and anything else needed to perform their duties as members of the force. When any Ranger made an arrest, he had to deliver his prisoner to the nearest marshal's office in the jurisdiction where the crime was committed.

The series, incidentally, was shot on location in Arizona, and many residents of Tulsa and Phoenix played supporting roles.

Tris Coffin died on March 26, 1990.

Dale Robertson

82

TALES OF WELLS FARGO

Starring Dale Robertson

CREDITS:

NBC: March 18, 1957 through September 8, 1962 (167 episodes); Produced by: Revue Productions/Overland Productions; Executive Producer: Nat Holt; Producer: Earle Lyon; Creators: Gene Reynolds, James Brooks; Directors: Jerry Hopper, R.G. Springsteen, Gene Reynolds; Music: Michael Greene, Melvin Lenard, Morton Stevens; Theme: Michael Greene, Stanley Wilson; Narrator: Dale Robertson.

CAST:

Jim Hardie	Dale Robertson
Jeb Gaine	William Demarest
Beau McCloud	Jack Ging
Ovie	Virginia Christine

Tales of Wells Fargo told of Jim Hardie, a special investigator and troubleshooter for Wells Fargo during the gold rush period of the 1860s.

Wells Fargo, a stageline transporting gold shipments across the Western Frontier, was plagued with holdups and robberies. Anyone who tampered with company shipments could expect to see unofficial lawman Jim Hardie on his trail.

The show evolved from "A Tale of Wells Fargo" with Dale Robertson, a 1956 segment of *Schlitz Playhouse of Stars*.

During the 1961 season run, *Tales of Wells Fargo* was expanded from thirty to sixty minutes and added new characters to the show. Hardie was now owner of a ranch outside San Francisco; Beau McCloud, his young assistant; and crusty Jeb Gaine, his foreman. The ranch next door was owned by the widow Ovie, who lived with her two attractive daughters. This series kept viewer attention for more than five years.

William Demarest died December 28, 1983.

Dale Robertson in *Tales of Wells Fargo*

Will Hutchins

SUGARFOOT

Starring Will Hutchins

CREDITS:

ABC: September 17, 1957 through July 3, 1961 (69 episodes); Produced by: Warner Brothers Television; Executive Producer: William T. Orr; Producers: Harry Tatelman, Carroll Case, Burt Dunne; Directors: Lee Sholem, Robert Altman, Leslie H. Martinson, Paul Henried, William Hall, Richard L. Bare; Music: Paul Sawtell; Theme: Mack David, Jerry Livingston.

CAST:

Sugarfoot, Tom Brewster	Will Hutchins
Canary Kid	Will Hutchins
Toothy Thompson	Jack Elam

One of the better Westerns to come out of the Warner Brothers corral was *Sugarfoot*, a classic of the genre, running nearly four years.

It was the story of a steely-eyed cowboy who usually ambled his way into every kind of trouble possible. His

Will Hutchins as *Sugarfoot*

Will Hutchins shown here in a dual role from an episode entitled, "The Canary Kid."

Will Hutchins in *Sugarfoot*

Logo from *Sugarfoot*

name was Tom Brewster, otherwise known as "Sugarfoot." Sugar-what? I know what some of you young whippersnappers are asking; well, in the Old West, a sugarfoot was one step lower than a tenderfoot, meaning the cowboy was a greenhorn, not rugged enough for the Wild West. However, do not be mistaken by lackadaisical Tom Brewster's deceptively easygoing personality, or you might be staring down the barrel of his Colt .45 or lassoed by his quick roping action. That was what most town bullies and troublemakers encountered when messing with this mild-mannered character.

Brewster only had one interest in life, with the exception of the pretty ladies he met while roaming around the West: He was studying law through a correspondence course. Somehow he found little time to pursue his dream of being a lawyer because someone was always asking for a little help. The little help always meant a whole lot of trouble for Sugarfoot, I mean Tom Brewster.

Will Hutchins

James Garner and Jack Kelly

MAVERICK

Starring James Garner and Jack Kelly

CREDITS:

ABC: September 22, 1957 through July 8, 1962 (124 episodes); Produced by: Warner Brothers Television; Executive producer: William T. Orr; Producers: Roy Huggins, Howie Horwitz; Directors: Robert Altman, Budd Boetticher, André De Toth, Michael O'Herlihy, William F. Claxton, Arthur Lubin, Douglas Heyes, Lee Sholem; Creator: Roy Huggins; Music: David Buttolph, Paul Francis Webster.

CAST:

Bret Maverick	James Garner
Bart Maverick	Jack Kelly
Beau Maverick	Roger Moore
Brent Maverick	Robert Colbert
Samantha Crawford	Diane Brewster

Maverick was one of television's most popular shows about a character one would not soon forget. Bret

James Garner
in *Maverick*

Logo from *Maverick*

James Garner as
Bret and Jack Kelly
as Bart

Jack Kelly as Bart Maverick

Soon after *Maverick* began, Bret's equally adept brother Bart was introduced to the series. Bret and Bart alternated each week on the series and occasionally appeared together. Some of those episodes are considered classics today.

Maverick was different from other television Westerns. It became quite humorous at times, but still with an adult Western flavor. Neither Bret or Bart would have been given a medal for bravery, but they weren't exactly cowards either. However, the Maverick boys could be seen on more than one occasion sneaking out the back door or out of town if trouble erupted.

In 1960, James Garner walked out of the show over a contract dispute. A judge in Los Angeles ruled in Garner's favor, releasing him from his Warners contract, and he was replaced in the series with Roger Moore as Cousin Beauregard Maverick, a British relative. That didn't work too well, so the studio gave it one last go with Robert Colbert as Brent Maverick, a brother never before mentioned on the show. But *Maverick* kept on losing popularity, finally coming to an end on July 8, 1962, when *Maverick* dealt its last hand.

Jack Kelly died November 7, 1992.

Robert Colbert, Jack Kelly, and Roger Moore

Maverick drifted onto the television screen one Sunday night and gambled his way into the hearts of millions. A tall, handsome, semihonest gambler, he roamed through the West looking for poker games while trying to make a living at cards. Trouble always seemed to follow Maverick, but most of the time it was caused by the ladies, who used their feminine charms to embroil him. One thorn in his side was Samantha Crawford, a fake Southern Belle who frequently got Maverick into hot water with her conniving schemes.

HAVE GUN, WILL TRAVEL

Starring Richard Boone

CREDITS:

CBS: September 14, 1957 through September 21, 1963 (156 episodes); Executive Producer: Sam H. Rolfe; Producers: Frank Pierson, Don Ingalls, Robert Sparks; Directors: Robert Butler, Jerry Hopper, Ida Lupino, Richard Boone, Andrew V. McLaglen, Frank Pierson, Lamont Johnson; Music: Leith Stevens, Jeff Alexander, Bernard Herrmann, Jerry Goldsmith; Music: Richard Boone, Sam H. Rolfe; Theme Song Performer: Johnny Western.

Richard Boone

This top gun carried a business card and lived in a fancy hotel in San Francisco.

Richard Boone in *Have Gun, Will Travel*

Paladin's calling card

Richard Boone as Paladin and Kam Tong as Hey Boy, his servant

94

CAST:

Paladin . . . . Richard Boone
Hey Boy (servant) . . . . Kam Tong
Hey Girl (servant) . . . . Lisa-Lu
Mr. McGunnis (hotel manager) . . . Olan Soulé

Have Gun, Will Travel was among television's most popular Westerns. It was unique and seldom out of the top ten Nielsen ratings during its long successful run on CBS.

Perhaps the most debonair gun-for-hire was a man called only by his last name, Paladin, who lived in the finest hotel in San Francisco, the Hotel Carlton. Erudite, he ate the best food, dressed nattily, was always gentlemanly, enjoyed the opera, and carried a business card that read: HAVE GUN, WILL TRAVEL. WIRE PALADIN, SAN FRANCISCO.

Richard Boone as Paladin

Paladin's gun was not for hire to people on the wrong side of the law. He was the equalizer to those in distress who could no longer survive the lawlessness without professional help. Paladin was a gallant but tough hombre you didn't want to mess with, especially if you were a bad man. Paladin, a former United States Army officer in charge of weapons who had become disillusioned by the Civil War, decided to head West and dedicate himself to a better life by hiring out his gun as a soldier of fortune. His trademark, besides his distinctive business card, was the fancy black-leather holster of his gunbelt which bore the symbol of a Paladin (the white chess knight), also found on the rifle he used.

Richard Boone died January 10, 1981.

THE CALIFORNIANS

Starring Richard Coogan

CREDITS:

NBC: September 24, 1957 through August 27, 1959 (69 episodes); Produced by: Desilu Productions; Executive Producers: Louis F. Edelman, Robert F. Sisk; Producers: Robert Bassler, Felix Feist; Director: Felix Feist; Music: Harry Warren; Theme Song Performers: Ken Darby Singers.

CAST:

Marshal Mathew Wayne (from episode 23)	Richard Coogan
Dion Patrick (first 22 episodes)	Adam Kennedy
Jack McGivern	Sean McClory
Sam Brennan	Herbert Rudley
Jeremy Pitt	Arthur Fleming
Wilma Fansler	Carole Mathews
Martha McGivern	Nan Leslie

The Californians told of the exploits first of gold prospector-turned-reporter Dion Patrick, then of Marshal Matt Wayne, and their attempts to clean up then lawless San Francisco, which was overrun by crime during the Gold Rush period of the 1850s. Their nemesis was general-store owner Jack McGivern, who had taken over the city and with his vigilantes was searching for gold. The birth of any town has its various opposing factions, and San Francisco was no different.

Richard Coogan

96

Photo: Courtesy of TV Guide

Clint Walker in *Cheyenne*

John Payne in *The Restless Gun*

James Garner as Bret Maverick

Richard Boone in *Have Gun, Will Travel*

Guy Williams as *Zorro*

Chuck Connors and Johnny Crawford

George Montgomery in *Cimarron City*.

John Russell and Peter Brown in *Lawman*

Henry Fonda and Allen Case in *The Deputy*

Jock Mahoney and X Brands in *Yancy Derringer*

Nick Adams in *The Rebel*

Gene Barry in
Bat Masterson

*Photo:
Courtesy of TV Guide*

Clint Eastwood in *Rawhide*

Eric Fleming and Clint
Eastwood in *Rawhide*

Pernell Roberts, Michael Landon, Lorne Greene
and Dan Blocker in *Bonanza*

John Smith, Robert Fuller, Hoagy Carmichael, and Robert Crawford, Jr. in *Laramie*

Darren McGavin and Burt Reynolds in *Riverboat*

Dale Robertson in *The Iron Horse*

James Drury in *The Virginian*

(from left) Lee Majors, Peter Breck, Richard Long, Barbara
Stanwyck, and Linda Evans (seated) in *The Big Valley*

Richard Coogan in *The Californians*

Wayde Preston

Not long after *The Californians* began its first season, Adam Kennedy left the lead role in the series, and Richard Coogan took over as the star and rode it to the end of the trail.

Marshal Wayne organized a fifty-man law enforcement system to fight the rowdy gamblers, gold prospectors, and assorted vigilantes and varmints. He often found a moment of refuge from the politics and gunmen in the company of Wilma Fansler, a young widow who owned a local gambling house.

COLT .45

Starring Wayde Preston

CREDITS:

ABC: October 18, 1957 through September 27, 1960 (67 episodes); Produced by: Warner Brothers Television; Executive Producer: William T. Orr; Producers: Harry Tatleman, Roy Huggins, Cedric Francis, Joseph Hoffman, Mack David; Directors: Herbert L. Strock, Lew Landers, William Hale, Lee Sholem, Abner Biberman, Douglas Heyes, Walter Grauman, Marc Daniels; Music: Bert Shefter, Paul Sawtell; Theme: Mack David, Jerry Livingston.

CAST:

Christopher Colt	Wayde Preston
Sam Colt, Jr.	Donald May

Colt .45 was the story of Christopher Colt, a federal agent working undercover posing as a gun salesman to apprehend desperadoes wanted by the government during the 1880s. Chris Colt was part of the gunmaking family, which founded the Colt Firearms Company in Hartford, Connecticut. He wore a pair of Colt .45 single-action army revolvers, and used his Colt demonstrations and gun-selling business as a cover-up to track down army deserters, violent criminals, and tax cheats.

In the show's third season, Wayde Preston walked out of his starring role as Chris Colt after several disagreements with Warner Brothers. Preston claimed he was doing scenes which called for a stuntman and cited other problems concerning his show's low budget. Wayde Preston was replaced in 1960 by Donald May as Sam Colt, Jr., Christopher's cousin, who took over the lead till the show was canceled a few episodes

Wayde Preston in *Colt .45*

Wayde Preston as Christopher Colt

Wayde Preston returned in the 1959 season wearing a new mustache.

Logo from *Colt .45*

Wayde Preston as Chris Colt in action scene from *Colt .45*

Wayde Preston and guest star Roxanne Bernard in an episode entitled, "The Man Who Loved Lincoln"

later. After breaking his seven-year contract with Warners, Wayde Preston was not again seen on television except for one guest appearance on *NBC's The Hardy Boys Mystery*.

Wayde Preston died February 25, 1992.

ZORRO

Starring Guy Williams

CREDITS:

ABC: September 19, 1957 through September 24, 1959; Produced by: Walt Disney Productions: Producer: William N. Anderson; Directors: Norman Foster, William Witney, Hollingsworth Morse; Music: George Bruns; Theme: George Bruns, Norman Foster.

CAST:

Zorro/Don Diego	. . . .	Guy Williams
Bernardo	. . . .	Gene Sheldon
Captain Monastario	. . . . . .	Britt Lomond
Sergeant Garcia	. . . .	Henry Calvin

Who could ever forget that swashbuckling, black-garbed, and masked romantic hero who galloped into the hearts of millions with his rapier gleaming and his wit taunting. He was a mysterious man, known as Zorro, alias Don Diego, in Monterey, California, and these were his adventures.

The television story begins when Don Diego returns from Spain to Spanish California at his father's request, because a new ruler has placed the territory under martial law and is terrorizing the land owners and peons alike with brutality and excessive taxes. Don Diego poses as a lazy, foppish aristocrat unconcerned about local welfare to protect his secret identity as the masked avenger. His mission is to eradicate the evil reign of Captain Monastario and see that justice is served. To that end Zorro mounts a one-man crusade against the soldiers and their tyrannical leader.

With the thunder of hooves in the night, the flash of a sword, and the soldiers' barracks in mass confusion, the community knows that Zorro is once again at work on their behalf. His true identity was known only to his father's deaf-mute servant Bernardo, Zorro's loyal friend, who faithfully cares for the black stallion Tornado and Zorro's white stallion Phantom, both kept in secret locations for rapid escapes and the bafflement of the already bewildered soldiers of Captain Monastario.

But let us not forget the bumbling but lovable Sergeant Garcia, who always seemed to be going in several different directions at the same time while forever being branded with the mark of Zorro on various undignified parts of his body.

Guy Williams

In the early 1990s, a new *Zorro* series emerged on cable television. Starring in the title role was Canadian actor Duncan Regehr. His father was played initially by Efrem Zimbalist, Jr., and then by Henry Darrow.

Guy Williams died May 6, 1989.

TRACKDOWN

Starring Robert Culp

CREDITS:

CBS: October 4, 1957 through September 23, 1959; Produced by: Four Star Productions; Executive Producer: Vincent M. Fennelly; Director: Donald McDougall; Music: Herschel Burke Gilbert.

CAST:

Hoby Gilman	Robert Culp
Henrietta Porter	Ellen Corby
Ralph	Norman Leavitt

Robert Culp

Trackdown was a spin-off from *Dick Powell's Zane Grey Theatre* and based on the official files of the Texas Rangers. This Western series, set in the 1870s, told of the experiences of Ranger Hoby Gilman and his attempts to apprehend outlaws wanted by the Lone Star State. Tracking down criminals meant asking for help from law-abiding citizens. Gilman always could count on Henrietta Porter, editor of the newspaper in Porter, Texas, and Ralph, a handyman around town, to help him put the felons behind bars.

A number of episodes were either written or directed by star Robert Culp in this well-made Western series several years before he began *I Spy*.

TOMBSTONE TERRITORY

Starring Pat Conway

CREDITS:

ABC: October 16, 1957 through September 17, 1958; March 13, 1959 through October 9, 1959; Produced by:

Pat Conway as Sheriff Clay Hollister

ZIV Television Productions; Producers: Frank Pittman, Andy White; Theme song written and performed by: William Backer; Narrator: Richard Eastham.

CAST:

Sheriff Clay Hollister	Pat Conway
Harris Claibourne	Richard Eastham
Deputy Charlie Riggs	Gil Rankin

Tombstone Territory was another successful series released during the late 1950s when adult Westerns were in their prime. Although this series was canceled by the network in 1958, the show, in an unusual move at the time, continued in syndication with new episodes for quite some time.

It was a story of Tombstone, Arizona, "the town too tough to die," during the 1880s. Law and order was enforced by Sheriff Clay Hollister, who was quite capable of handling any kind of criminal activity. Tombstone was well known for its past history of wild cowboys, drifters, and shoot-outs like the O.K. Corral gunfight. Needless to say, the sheriff got little support from the town's business people in his struggle against violence. Hollister, on the other hand, did have one man in town who believed in his brand of law—Harris Claibourne, the editor of the local newspaper, "The Tombstone Epitaph." Claibourne used his "power of the press" to support the sheriff's policies.

Ward Bond and Robert Horton

WAGON TRAIN

Starring Ward Bond and Robert Horton

CREDITS:

NBC: September 18, 1957 through September 12, 1962, 252 black and white episodes: 60 minutes, and 32 color episodes: 90 minutes; ABC September 19, 1962 through September 5, 1965; Produced by: Revue Productions; Producers: Howard Christie, Richard Lewis; Directors: Bernard Girard, Don Weis, Gene Coon, Ted Post, Arnold Laven, John Ford, Virgil L. Vogel; Music: Richard Sendry, Hans Salter, Melvin Lenard; Theme: Jerome Moross.

CAST:

Major Seth Adams	Ward Bond
Flint McCullough	Robert Horton
Charlie Wooster	Frank McGrath
Bill Hawks	Terry Wilson
Chris Hale (1961–65)	John McIntire
Cooper Smith (1961–65) . . .	Robert Fuller
Duke Shannon (1961–65)	Denny Miller

Wagon Train was a blockbuster in television Westerns, owing a lot to John Ford's popular *Wagonmaster* (1950). Ford's friend Ward Bond, who was in the film, became the star of this long-running series.

It followed a wagon train heading west from Missouri to California during the 1870s. The trek was led by wagonmaster Major Seth Adams and his Indian scout Flint McCullough. Each story of the show was an emotional saga of wagon train passengers (big name guest stars) who endured many hardships on the route: deadly diseases, Indian attacks, and other misfortunes. There were few violent scenes in the show, and gunfights were played down, although you could expect one good action shoot-out at least in each episode. Some of the most enjoyable moments in

Wagon Train were the humorous scenes played out between gruff Major Adams and the cook Charlie Wooster. They never could agree on anything.

Ward Bond died in 1960 and was replaced by John McIntire as Chris Hale, the new wagonmaster. The show made a few changes in the cast when it returned for the 1961 season and went from sixty minutes in black and white to ninety in color.

Ward Bond died November 5, 1960.
Frank McGrath died May 13, 1967.
John McIntire died January 30, 1991.

Ward Bond as Maj. Seth Adams

Terry Wilson as Bill Hawks

John McIntire as Chris Hale took over as wagonmaster in the 1961 season following Ward Bond's death.

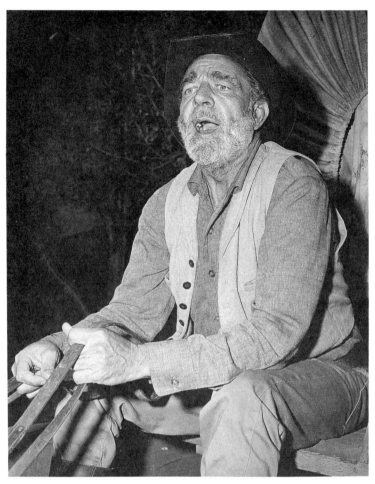

Frank McGrath as the lovable cook Charlie Wooster

FRONTIER DOCTOR

Starring Rex Allen

CREDITS:

Syndicated: 1957–59 (39 episodes); Produced by: Studio City Television Service; Producer: Edward J. White; Director: William Witney.

CAST:

Dr. Bill Baxter . . . . Rex Allen

Frontier Doctor depicted the life and times of a physician in the town of Rising Springs, Arizona, in the 1890s. Dr. Bill Baxter tried to enforce neglected medical laws and help the struggling pioneers in their efforts to eke out a minimal living under adverse conditions presented by nasty outlaws, unscrupulous land barons, and angry Indians.

The role of a doctor in those times often went beyond prescribing medicine, performing surgery, and dispensing medical advice. More often the doctor rather than the clergy had to be the backbone of the community, providing spiritual strength and establishing a high moral code.

Dr. Baxter, as played by white-hatted veteran cowboy Rex Allen, survivor of countless B Westerns, never carried a gun but did not hesitate to uphold justice and protect his patients from the lawless in those violent and turbulent times.

The series also was syndicated over the years as both *Man of the West* and *Unarmed*.

Myron Healey is held back from Rex Allen (left) in a scene from *Frontier Doctor.*

This Western depicted the life of an unusual Mexican-American sheriff/lawyer, Elfego Baca, who pulled

THE NINE LIVES OF ELFEGO BACA

Starring Robert Loggia

CREDITS:

ABC: October 3, 1958 through June 17, 1959 (10 episodes); Produced by: Walt Disney Productions; Executive producer: Walt Disney; Producer: James Pratt; Director: Norman Foster; Music: William Lava; Theme song: Richard Dehr, Frank Miller.

CAST:

Sheriff Elfego Baca . . . . . . Robert Loggia

The Nine Lives of Elfego Baca was shown in segments as part of the *Walt Disney Presents* series. The show was based on a true story of a fearless, 1880s lawman in Socorro County, New Mexico.

Robert Loggia

his gun only on the side of the law. What made Baca so unusual was the fact that he seldom ever shot a varmint, yet he was feared by outlaws because of a past incident that spread his name throughout the untamed West.

Baca once held off a lynch mob of eighty cowboys, who fired four thousand rounds of ammunition into an old shack where he was hiding, and he escaped without a scratch. The Mexican-Americans, whose lives he defended, called Baca "The Unkillable Man." As his scare tactic, Sheriff Baca wrote a letter to each outlaw he was after, warning them if they did not surrender themselves by a certain time, they would have to face him. Needless to say, the ploy worked.

TEXAS JOHN SLAUGHTER

Starring Tom Tryon

CREDITS:

ABC: October 31, 1958 through April 23, 1961 (15 episodes shown periodically over nearly three years); Produced by: Walt Disney Productions; Executive Producer: Walt Disney; Producer: James Pratt; Director: Harry Keller; Music: Buddy Baker; Theme written and performed by: Stan Jones.

CAST:

Texas John Slaughter	Tom Tryon
Viola Slaughter	Betty Lynn
Willie Slaughter	Brian Corcoran

This series eventually presented a rounded version of Texas John Slaughter's life, based on the true story of a Western hero.

Texas John Slaughter, a Texas Ranger who became sheriff in Friotown, Texas, during the 1880s, dedicated his time to maintaining the law there. Slaughter's reputation was well known as was his remarkable ability at fisticuffs and lightning-fast cross-handed draw. Slaughter, an expert shot and judge of men, never hesitated to deliver a verdict with Mr. Colt.

Tom Tryon, who left acting to become a bestselling novelist, died September 4, 1991.

Tom Tryon as Texas John Slaughter

THE RIFLEMAN

Starring Chuck Connors and Johnny Crawford

CREDITS:

ABC: September 30, 1958 through July 1, 1963 (168 episodes); Produced by: Four Star Productions; Producers: Jules Levy, Arthur Gardner, Arnold Laven; Directors: Sam Peckinpah, Arnold Laven, Arthur Hiller, Tom Gries, Don Taylor, Ida Lupino, Lamont Johnson, Lewis Allen; Music: Herschel Burke Gilbert.

CAST:

Lucas McCain	Chuck Connors
Mark McCain	Johnny Crawford
Marshal Micah Torrance	Paul Fix
Lou Mallory	Patricia Blair

Millie Scott	Joan Taylor
Hattie Denton	Hope Summers
Sweeney, the bartender	Bill Quinn

One of the most exciting Westerns during the 1950s was *The Rifleman*. It was unusual and action-packed, which is why this show remains a favorite today in reruns being shown throughout the world.

The Rifleman told the story of stalwart Lucas McCain, a widower who attempted to raise his young son Mark into manhood. The McCains lived on a small cattle spread located outside of North Fork, New Mexico, a town that had its share of outlaws, town bullies, rustlers, and gunslingers. Many of the lawless troublemakers who rode into North Fork never rode out. They were buried there after challenging Lucas McCain's 44.40 Winchester rifle. He was deadly accurate in firing six rounds in four-tenths of a second with his modified rifle, the trigger being tripped by a screw on the guard. He only needed to cock the rifle once, (usually in a twirl) to fire twelve shots. One shot was eliminated and edited from the original opening of the show.

Micah Torrance, the ineffective town marshal, called on Lucas for his assistance in apprehending the villains in North Fork when things heated up, which happened quite often. Other highly respected citizens in town were Miss Millie Scott, who owned the general store, and Miss Lou Mallory, McCain's romantic interest and the owner of the Mallory Hotel.

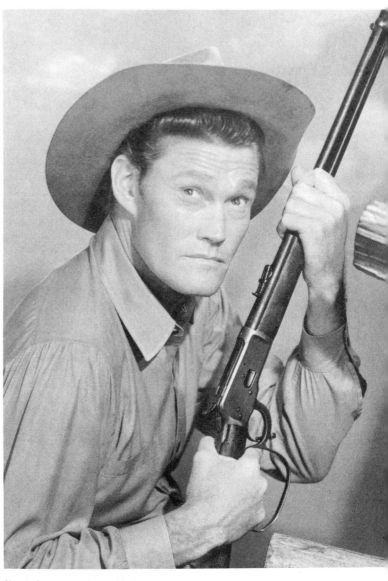

Chuck Connors as Lucas McCain

Chuck Connors

Chuck Connors as Lucas McCain, the Rifleman

Paul Fix as Marshal Micah Torrance, the lawman in Northfork, New Mexico.

In 1991, Connors and a now grown Crawford reprised their *Rifleman* roles in Kenny Rogers's stellar television Western *The Gambler Returns: The Luck of the Draw*.

Chuck Connors died November 10, 1992.

Paul Fix died October 14, 1983.

JEFFERSON DRUM

Starring Jeff Richards

CREDITS:

NBC: April 25, 1958 through April 23, 1959 (26 episodes); Produced by: Goodson-Todman Productions; Executive Producer: Matthew Rapf; Producers: Mark Goodson, Bill Todman.

CAST:

Jefferson Drum	Jeff Richards
Joey Drum	Eugene Martin
Lucius Coin	Cyril Delevanti
Big Ed	Robert Stevenson

The thirty-minute Western series *Jefferson Drum* was about the crusading editor of a newspaper called "The Star" in a tough and tumble gold-mining town, Jubilee, during the 1850s. Drum proved he could aim a Colt revolver as well as an editorial at the town's lawless elements. A courageous man who stood beside the sheriff in protecting the citizens of the tough Western community, Drum used his "power of the press" to fight corruption and crooked politicians. Lucius Coin, Drum's printer, and Big Ed the bartender were also ready to help when trouble came calling. Jefferson Drum was a widower and attempted to raise his young son Joey, who could be seen playing around the newspaper office while dad was working.

Jefferson Drum was one of several dramatic series put together by game-show producers Goodson and Todman.

Jeff Richards died July 28, 1989.

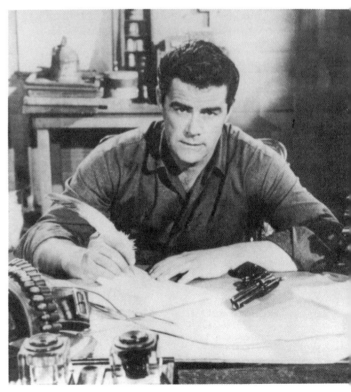

Jeff Richards

THE ROUGH RIDERS

Starring Kent Taylor

CREDITS:

ABC: October 2, 1958 through September 24, 1959 (39 episodes); Produced by: ZIV Television Productions; Producer: Andy White.

(From left) Jan Merlin, Kent Taylor, and Peter Whitney

CAST:

Capt. Jim Flagg	Kent Taylor
Lt. Colin Kirby	Jan Merlin
Sgt. Buck Sinclair	Peter Whitney

The series revolved around the three men called "The Rough Riders" who traveled west during the 1860s following the Civil War. After their discharge from the service, two Union soldiers, Capt. Jim Flagg and Sgt. Buck Sinclair, joined forces with a Confederate officer, Lt. Colin Kirby, to journey to the frontier to begin new lives.

The trio traded gunfire with infamous outlaws while searching the Dakota Badlands and other Indian territories looking for that special place to hang up their spurs. During their weekly adventures, the Rough Riders crossed paths with numerous outlaw bands, renegade Indians, and deserters from both armies; aided victims of injustice; and were always gallant toward the ladies. The Rough Riders were an imposing team but should not be confused with Teddy Roosevelt's band of Spanish-American War heroes charging down the slopes of San Juan Hill.

The trio's search west for security and personal identity was a recurring theme in many Western novels and television series.

Kent Taylor died April 11, 1987.

LAWMAN

Starring John Russell and Peter Brown

CREDITS:

ABC: October 5, 1958 through October 9, 1962; Produced by: Warner Brothers Television; Executive Producer: William T. Orr; Producers: Jules Schermer,

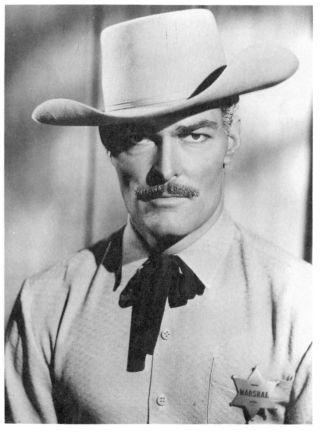

John Russell

111

Charles Trapnell; Directors: Richard Sarafian, Lee Sholem, Leslie H. Martinson, Burt Kennedy, Richard L. Bare, Robert Altman; Music: Mack David, Jerry Livingston.

CAST:

Marshal Dan Troop	John Russell
Deputy Johnny McKay	Peter Brown
Lilly Merrill	Peggie Castle
Jake, the bartender	Dan Sheridan

One of television's most exciting Westerns was *Lawman*, following the exploits of rugged Marshal Dan Troop and his deputy Johnny McKay as they enforced law and order in the town of Laramie, Wyoming, during the 1870s. Troop was a tough, taciturn marshal and stood firm upholding the law, accepting no substitutes for justice, nor was he afraid of any two-bit gunslinger with a big reputation.

Lawman was obviously Warners' attempt to simulate the success and thrust of *Gunsmoke*. Each had a stalwart, somewhat stoic cowboy star. And just as *Gunsmoke's* Matt Dillon had Miss Kitty running the Long Branch Saloon, *Lawman's* Dan Troop had a similar relationship with Miss Lilly, proprietor of the Birdcage Saloon. Dan Troop and his young deputy (who always addressed his boss as "Mr. Troop") protected Laramie and its citizens for a successful four-year run.

John Russell died January 29, 1991.
Peggie Castle died August 11, 1973.

Robert Clark (left) guest stars with John Russell and Peter Brown in *Lawman* episode entitled, "The Last Man."

Logo from *Lawman*

John Russell as Marshal Dan Troop and Peter Brown as Deputy Johnny McKay in *Lawman*

John Russell and Peggie Castle

CIMARRON CITY

Starring George Montgomery

CREDITS:

NBC: October 11, 1958 through September 26, 1959 (26 episodes); Produced by: Revue Productions; Executive Producer: Richard Lewis; Producers: Felix Jackson, Norman Jolly, Boris Ingster, Richard Bartlett; Director: Jules Bricken; Narrator: George Montgomery.

George Montgomery and John Smith

113

CAST:

Matt Rockford	. . . . .	George Montgomery
Lane Temple	. . . .	John Smith
Beth Purcell	. . . .	Audrey Totter
Tiny Budinger	. . . .	Dan Blocker
Art Sampson	. . . .	Stuart Randall
Alice Purdy	. . . .	Claire Carleton

Perhaps one of the best titles for a Western had to be any show using the name Cimarron, as was the title of this series, *Cimarron City*.

Cimarron City was the story of the famed Oklahoma frontier town during the 1880s, an oil and gold mining center attracting every gunman and cowpoke to its booming growth. Stalwart Matt Rockford, mayor of Cimarron City, which his father had founded, was highly respected by the town's leading citizens. Rockford was also a well-loved cattle baron who involved himself in the problems of the local ranchers, the townsfolk, and the strangers passing through.

Other upstanding citizens in the town were Lane Temple, sheriff of Cimmaron City; Beth Purcell, Matt Rockford's romantic interest; and handyman and jack-of-all-trades Tiny Budinger.

Dan Blocker died May 14, 1972.

George Montgomery as Matt Rockford in *Cimarron City*

George Montgomery
as Matt Rockford

John Smith in *Cimarron City*

BAT MASTERSON

Starring Gene Barry

CREDITS:

NBC: October 8, 1958 through September 21, 1961 (108 episodes); Produced by: ZIV Television Productions; Producers: Andy White, Frank Pittman; Narrator: Bill Baldwin; Directors: Lew Landers, Walter Doniger, Eddie Davis, Montgomery Pittman.

CAST:

Bat Masterson . . . . Gene Barry

Bat Masterson was a story about a man who became a legend in the Old West during the 1880s. William Barclay Masterson had been a well-respected sheriff of Dodge City, Kansas, earning himself a famous reputation as a lawman. The citizens of Dodge City presented Bat with a custom-made nickel-plated Colt .45 for their appreciation of his services.

> "Back when the West was very young,
> There lived a man named Masterson;
> He wore a cane and derby hat,
> They called him Bat, Bat Masterson."

So went the title song introducing the show.

Following his days as lawman, Bat turned professional gambler and wandering law enforcer, traveling the West carrying his gold-tipped cane and wearing a derby hat, his trademark. The suave Bat Masterson was considered a gentleman gambler and also quite charming with the ladies. Bat traveled mostly between Kansas and California plying his trade, trusting in Lady Luck, but still having high respect for the law.

Gene Barry

Gene Barry in *Bat Masterson*

116

Gene Barry as Bat Masterson

Gene Barry in a scene from *Bat Masterson*

MacKENZIE'S RAIDERS

Starring Richard Carlson

CREDITS:

Syndicated: 1958–59 (39 episodes); Produced by ZIV Television Productions; Producer: Barney Slater.

CAST:

Col. Ranald S. MacKenzie . . .	Richard Carlson
Raiders	Louis Jean Heydt
	Jack Ging
	Jim Bridges
	Brett King
	Charles Boax
	Kenneth Alton

MacKenzie's Raiders was set in Texas during the 1870s and told of the exploits of dashing Col. Ranald S.

Richard Carlson

Richard Carlson in *MacKenzie's Raiders*

YANCY DERRINGER

Starring Jock Mahoney

CREDITS:

CBS: October 2, 1958 through September 24, 1959 (34 episodes); Produced by: Desilu Productions; Executive Producers: Don Sharpe, Warren Lewis; Producers: Richard Sale, Mary Loos, A. E. Houghton; Directors: William F. Claxton, Richard Sale; Music: Leon Klatskin; Theme Song: Don Quinn, Henry Russell.

CAST:

Yancy Derringer	Jock Mahoney
Pahoo-Ka-Ta-Wha	X Brands
John Colton	Kevin Hagen
Madame Francine	Frances Bergen
Jody Barker	Richard Devon
Captain Fry	Robert McCord III

Yancy Derringer was an adventure series that had a unique style of action in an exciting Louisiana setting

Jock Mahoney

MacKenzie, a commander of the U.S. Fourth Cavalry working as an undercover agent with secret orders from the President of the United States. Maurauding Mexican renegades had taken over the Texas Territory, and the only way to end the terror was to form a special band of handpicked troopers. They would be called MacKenzie's Raiders, and they galloped forth week after week, alternating between stealthy attacks and displays of flashing swords, in this often rousing horse opera.

Col. Ranald S. MacKenzie was recognized as one of the most courageous heros in U.S. Army history. This television series was based on the book *The MacKenzie Raid* by Col. Russell Reeder.

Richard Carlson died November 25, 1977.

118

YANCY DERRINGER

Jock Mahoney and X Brands in *Yancy Derringer*

Kevin Hagen, Julie Adams, and Jock Mahoney in a scene from *Yancy Derringer*

Jock Mahoney in *Yancy Derringer*

BUCKSKIN

Starring Tommy Nolan

CREDITS:

NBC: July 3, 1958 through September 25, 1959 (39 episodes) (Repeated in summer 1965); Produced by: Revue Productions; Producer: Robert Bassler; Music: Stanley Wilson, Mort Green; Narrator: Tommy Nolan.

CAST:

Jody O'Connell	. . . .	Tommy Nolan
Annie O'Connell	. . . .	Sallie Brophy
Sheriff Tom Sellers	. . . .	Mike Road
Ben Newcombe, the		
schoolteacher	. . . .	Michael Lipton

Tommy Nolan

during the 1880s. Yancy Derringer, an ex-Confederate soldier from pre-Civil War days, is now a gambler who owns a riverboat called "The Sultana." He is also an undercover agent for the city of New Orleans administrator John Colton. The two struggle to enforce law and order in a city known for crime and corruption.

Yancy was known for his easy ways. He always traveled with the ladies and his mute bodyguard and Indian friend, Pahoo-Ka-Ta-Wha, an expert with gun and knife. Yancy's romantic interest was Madame Francine who owned a sporting club in New Orleans. (She was played by Candice "Murphy Brown" Bergen's mother, Frances Bergen.) Jody Barker, a professional pickpocket, added humor to the show as Yancy's informant.

Jock Mahoney died December 14, 1989.

Sallie Brophy and Mike Road in *Buckskin*

Buckskin was the story of Jody O'Connell, a ten-year-old boy living on the frontier with his widowed mother Annie, and growing up during the 1880s in the lawless territory of Buckskin, Montana. Annie operated a boardinghouse in town while attempting to protect her son and property from many shady characters who passed through Buckskin where Sheriff Tom Sellers kept law and order despite local residents whooping it up and causing more trouble than outsiders. Annie's main concern was for Jody to have a decent life and get a good education, even in a town with a wild side. Jody narrated each episode while sitting on a corral fence and playing his harmonica—tales of struggle in a lawless territory.

THE TEXAN

Starring Rory Calhoun

CREDITS:

CBS: September 29, 1958 through September 12, 1960 (80 episodes); Produced by: Rorvic-Desilu Productions; Executive Producer: William T. Orr; Producers: Rory Calhoun, Jerry Stagg, Vic Orsatti; Director: Alvin Ganzer; Narrator: Rory Calhoun.

CAST:

Bill Longley . . . . Rory Calhoun

Rory Calhoun

The Texan, an exciting Western series which starred Rory Calhoun, was based loosely on the real character Bill Longley, one of the West's most vicious outlaws. Longley, however, was a good guy in this popular Western. Calhoun not only starred in the series but also produced and narrated the eighty episodes shown on CBS (and later rerun on ABC).

The series was about the exploits of Bill Longley, a tall Texan, who wandered through the Texas Panhandle, usually helping people in distress, during the 1870s. Longley, an ex-gunfighter, frequently met trouble on his journeys, having to prove to another cowboy that he still was a little quicker on the trigger than expected.

The real Bill Longley, a wanted killer, was hanged in Galveston, Texas, on October 11, 1878.

Rory Calhoun in *The Texan*

Rory Calhoun as Bill Longley in a scene from *The Texan*

Ty Hardin

BRONCO

Starring Ty Hardin

CREDITS:

ABC: September 12, 1958 through September 20, 1960 (68 episodes); Produced by: Warner Brothers Television; Executive Producer: William T. Orr; Producers: Arthur Silver, Charles Hoffman, Steve Riddel, Bruce Dunn; Directors: Richard Sinclair, Leslie H. Martinson, Lee Sholem, Michael O'Herlihy, Lew Landers, André De Toth, Robert Altman, Leslie Goodwins; Music: Paul Sawtell; Theme: Mack David, Jerry Livingston.

CAST:

Bronco Layne	Ty Hardin
Toothy Thompson	Jack Elam

Ty Hardin in *Bronco*

Ty Hardin as Bronco Layne

Bronco was a television Western loaded with action and adventure. Its star (one of the class of fifties Warner heartthrobs) had big shoes to fill when he signed on as the lead in *Cheyenne,* one of television's most popular cowboy series. In 1958, Ty Hardin replaced Clint Walker when the latter walked out during a contract dispute with Warners. It wasn't until 1959 that Walker reached an agreement with the studio and returned to his show. *Bronco* then became a spin-off series on its own.

It was the story of Bronco Layne, a two-fisted ex-Confederate Army captain, who wandered the frontier during the post-Civil War period fighting injustice and outlaws. Bronco was a loner who preferred to avoid

Ty Hardin as Bronco in action

trouble, but when he couldn't, he stood firm and looked it square in the eye. He had had his share of trouble and despair after returning to Texas to find himself stripped of honor and his home confiscated. Bronco traveled the length and breadth of Texas helping people in distress and working at assorted jobs: secret missions for the federal government, a deputy sheriff, or a ranch hand. In his wanderings Bronco chased not only bad guys and Indians but a few charming ladies as well.

MAN WITHOUT A GUN

Starring Rex Reason

CREDITS:

Syndicated: April 1957 through January 1959; Produced by: 20th Century-Fox Television; Producers: Peter Packer, Alan A. Armer, Mel Epstein; Director: John H. Peyser, Christian Nyby; Music: Lionel Newman.

Rex Reason

CAST:

Adam MacLean . . . . Rex Reason
Marshal Frank Tallman . . . . . . Mort Mills

Man Without a Gun detailed the career of Adam MacLean, a crusading newspaper editor in Yellowstone, Dakota, during the 1870s. MacLean disliked guns and attempted to establish peace with his "Gunless West" policy through the power of the press. He published many stories in his newspaper, "The Yellowstone Sentinel," campaigning against carrying a six-gun, and Marshal Frank Tallman, the town lawman, supported his friend Adam MacLean's gunless policy. The two, though, found that gunslingers were not fond of giving up their gunbelts, thus creating the tension necessary for exciting drama, punctuated by lots of fisticuffs.

U.S. MARSHAL

Starring John Bromfield

CREDITS:

Syndicated: September 1958 through September 1960 (78 episodes); Produced by: Desilu Productions, Na-

John Bromfield as Marshal Frank Morgan

tional Telefilm Associates; Executive Producer: Mort Briskin; Producer: John H. Auer; Directors: Earl Bellamy, Harold Shuster, Robert Altman.

CAST:

Marshal Frank Morgan	John Bromfield
Deputy Tom Ferguson	James Griffith
Deputy Blake	Robert Brubaker
Deputy Rafe Peterson	
(earlier episodes)	Stan Jones

One of the very infrequent times in television history that a show changed titles but the main character remained the same occurred during the late 1950s in the case of *U.S. Marshal*. Initially it was called *The Sheriff of Cochise* (1956–58). John Bromfield, who starred as Sheriff Frank Morgan, was promoted to *U.S. Marshal* in 1958 after the sponsor, Anheuser-Busch, persuaded the producers and the studio to change the title of the show for better marketing purposes. The transition proved to be successful and Desilu Productions filmed a total of seventy-eight episodes of *U.S. Marshal* between 1958 and 1960 for syndicated television.

John Bromfield and James Griffith

126   Dan Blocker as Hoss Cartwright

U.S. Marshal was the story of Frank Morgan, law enforcement officer in Cochise County, Arizona, during the 1950s. This tough, modern-day lawman chased most of the bad guys in a new Dodge station wagon, but occasionally took to the hills on horseback in hot pursuit of a crook trying to escape to higher ground searching for a hideout. By either means, Morgan always caught his man with help from his reliable deputy Tom Ferguson. Together they closed all cases in the exciting *U.S. Marshal* episodes.

BONANZA

Starring Lorne Greene, Pernell Roberts, Dan Blocker, and Michael Landon

CREDITS:

NBC: September 12, 1959 through January 16, 1973 (440 episodes); Produced by: Paramount Television; Producers: Richard Collins, David Dortort, Robert Blees; Creator: David Dortort; Directors: Don Richardson, Lee H. Katzin, Christian I. Nyby, William Witney, Virgil W. Vogel, William F. Claxton; Music: David Rose, Harry Sukman, Raoul Kraushaar; Theme: Jay Livingston, Ray Evans.

Lorne Greene

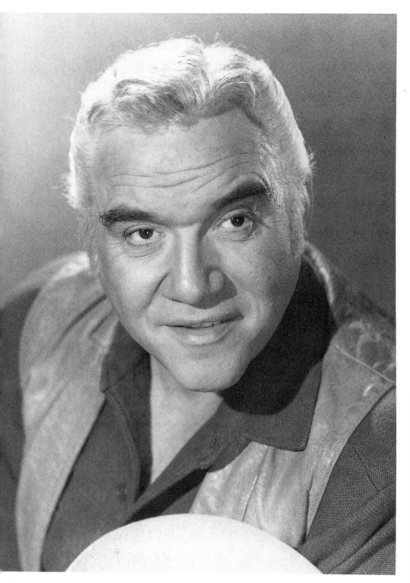

Lorne Greene as Ben Cartwright

CAST:

Ben Cartwright . . . . Lorne Greene
Adam Cartwright . . . . . . Pernell Roberts
Eric "Hoss" Cartwright . . . . . Dan Blocker
Little Joe Cartwright . . . . . Michael Landon
Hop Sing (house boy) . . . . Victor Sen Yung
Sheriff Roy Coffee . . . . Ray Teal
Mr. Canaday (ranch foreman) . . David Canary

In 1959, the Cartwrights rode into Virginia City to the strains of Jay Livingston and Ray Evans's immortal theme, in one of television's most popular adult Westerns, *Bonanza*. However, in the first season the Cartwrights failed to impress the Nielsen ratings or the viewers, but they loaded up their guns again for a second shot and galloped into television history over

Michael Landon as Little Joe

fourteen seasons, the second-longest-running Western series after *Gunsmoke*.

It followed the exploits of Ben Cartwright, a widower, and his sons Adam, Hoss, and Little Joe (all from different wives). The four men struggled to protect their 1,000-acre ranch, the Ponderosa, located near Virginia City, Nevada, in the 1850s. The Ponderosa was in the center of Nevada's Comstock Lode country, the site where the greatest deposit of silver ore was discovered. That usually meant trouble in most places, and this town was no exception, causing many problems for the Cartwrights. There were always desperadoes, cattle rustlers, escaped killers, scoundrels eyeing water rights and railroad rights-of-way, and conniving souls wandering onto the Ponderosa. The Cartwrights were a close-knit family and were always ready to help other people in distress.

Dan Blocker, Lorne Greene, Pernell Roberts, and Michael Landon in *Bonanza*

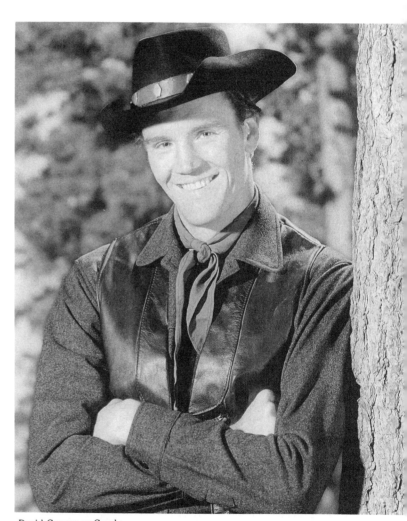

David Canary as Candy

129

Bonanza's success formula was that it depended more on character development and resolution of personal conflict than the traditional violent conclusion to problems. Top-name guest stars added to the show's drama and popularity.

Lorne Greene died September 11, 1987.
Dan Blocker died May 14, 1972.
Michael Landon died July 1, 1991.

WANTED: DEAD OR ALIVE

Starring Steve McQueen

CREDITS:

CBS: September 6, 1959 through September 22, 1961 (94 episodes); Produced by: Four Star Productions; Producers: John Robinson, Ed Adamson, Harry Harris;

Steve McQueen in *Wanted: Dead or Alive*

Directors: Richard Donner, Thomas Carr, George Blair, Gene Reynolds, Murray Golden, Ed Adamson; Music: Harry King, Herschel Burke Gilbert; Theme: Rudy Schrager.

CAST:

Josh Randall . . . . Steve McQueen

Wanted: Dead or Alive, which made a star of Steve McQueen, remains a favorite in reruns today though it was first viewed in 1959. This series was a spin-off from an episode of another television Western, *Trackdown*.

The setting was the frontier in the 1880s when bounty hunters were not liked by either lawmen or town citizens. This didn't matter to Josh Randall, who apprehended anyone having a price on his head and wanted by the law, dead or alive. Randall, a man of few words, brought in many outlaws in this action-packed series. He would ride into town, check out the wanted posters, and begin his search. One interesting feature in this show was Josh Randall's gun, a custom-made .30-.40-caliber sawed-off Winchester carbine, his "Mare's Laig", which he wore on his side like a handgun and could be fired with blazing speed.

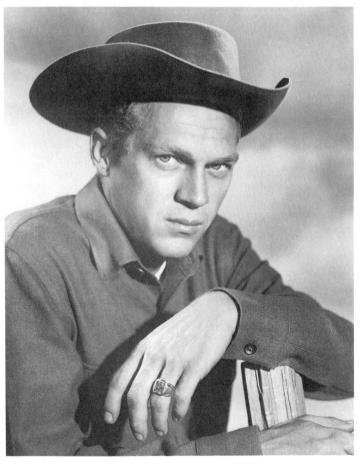

Steve McQueen

Interestingly, thirty-five years after *Wanted: Dead or Alive* left network television, an ultraviolent theatrical movie of the same title, set in modern times, had actor Rutger Hauer playing the bounty-hunting grandson of Josh Randall.

Steve McQueen died November 7, 1980.

THE DEPUTY

Starring Henry Fonda and Allen Case

CREDITS:

NBC: September 12, 1959 through September 16, 1961 (78 episodes); Produced by: Top Gun Productions, Revue Productions; Executive Producer: William Frye; Producers: Roland Kibbee, Michael Kraike; Creators: Roland Kibbee, Norman Lear; Directors: David Butler, Tay Garnett, Herschel Daugherty, Sidney Lanfield, Arthur Lubin; Music: Jack Marshall; Narrator: Henry Fonda.

Henry Fonda and Allen Case in *The Deputy*

CAST:

Marshal Simon Fry	Henry Fonda
Deputy Clay McCord	Allen Case
Marshal Herk Lamson	
(first season)	Wallace Ford
Fran McCord (first season) . . .	Betty Lou Keim
Sgt. Hapgood Tasker	
(second season)	Read Morgan

Movie legend Henry Fonda decided to give television a try in this 1959 Western series *The Deputy*. Unfortunately, he only appeared in every third episode, therefore explaining the title of this series. Allen Case, who played the deputy, tried to carry the show, but the viewers wanted more of Fonda.

The Deputy was the story of Marshal Simon Fry and part-time deputy Clay McCord maintaining law and order in Silver City, Arizona, during the 1880s. Marshal Fry was a dedicated, no-nonsense lawman who had little mercy for lawbreakers and was afraid of nothing. Clay McCord, a local storekeeper and expert with a gun, preferred to settle arguments with words instead of bullets. Although a pacifist, McCord kept peace in Silver City while Marshal Fry was patroling the Arizona Territory on his assignments.

Henry Fonda died August 12, 1982.

Allen Case died August 25, 1986.

LAW OF THE PLAINSMAN

Starring Michael Ansara

CREDITS:

NBC: October 1, 1959 through September 22, 1960 (30 episodes); Produced by: Four Star Productions; Executive Producers: Jules Levy, Arthur Gardner, Arnold Laven; Producers: Peter Packer, Arthur Nadel; Directors: James Neilson, Paul Wendkos, William F. Claxton, John Peyser; Music: Leonard Rosenman.

CAST:

Marshal Sam Buckhart	Michael Ansara
Billy Lordan	Robert Harland
Tess Logan (Sam's ward)	Gina Gillespie

In *The Law of the Plainsman*, the star did not have a

fancy gun nor did he wear fancy clothes nor was he a famous gunfighter. What was unique was the fact that the main character was a Harvard-educated Apache Indian and a United States Marshal. Ethnic-looking Michael Ansara, who earlier had starred as Cochise in *Broken Arrow*, played the lead. This series, set in the 1880s in the wild New Mexico Territory, was a spin-off from an episode of *The Rifleman*, which drew lots of interest from television viewers.

Sam Buckhart was based in Santa Fe, where he was assigned to a territory to maintain law and order and, as an Indian lawman, he faced twice as many problems. He often found prejudice and hostility among the white men when attempting to apprehend the bad guys. Marshal Buckhart had high respect for the white man's law but never forgot his heritage or beliefs.

Michael Ansara in *Law of the Plainsman*

Michael Ansara

JOHNNY RINGO

Starring Don Durant

CREDITS:

CBS: October 2, 1959 through September 5, 1960 (38 episodes); Produced by: Four Star Productions; Executive Producer: Aaron Spelling; Producer: Stephen Lord; Creator: Aaron Spelling; Directors: Lamont Johnson, Larry Stewart, Don Taylor, David Lowell Rich, Paul Henried, Howard W. Koch; Music: Rudy Schrager, Laurindo Almeida; Theme song written and performed by: Don Durant.

CAST:

Johnny Ringo	Don Durant
Cully Charlcey	Mark Goddard
Laura Thomas	Karen Sharpe
Cason "Case" Thomas . . .	Terence DeMarney

Johnny Ringo was the story of a famous gunslinger who became sheriff in the town of Velardi, Arizona, during the 1880s, trying to forget about his violent past. However, every gunfighter who came through Velardi wanted to try Ringo's draw. It had been said "No one had ever beaten Ringo's hand." Most of those outlaws who rode into Velardi didn't ride out.

Soon after Ringo became sheriff, a young gunslinger named Cully Charlcey came to town with a Wild West show. He claimed to be the fastest gun in the West. He never left town with the show; he stayed and became Ringo's deputy.

Johnny Ringo wore a custom-made six shooter, only this six-gun had a special cylinder that fired an extra shot. The shot was a single shotgun shell fired through a modified short barrel beneath the gun's long barrel. This often surprised Ringo's opponents when they thought he was out of ammunition. The gun was called the "Le Mat Special."

Ringo's romantic interest in the show was the beautiful Laura Thomas, who worked at Velardi's General Store owned by her father.

The pilot for this series was shown as "The Loner" in spring 1959 on *Dick Powell's Zane Grey Theatre*.

Don Durant in *Johnny Ringo*

RAWHIDE

Starring Eric Fleming and Clint Eastwood

CREDITS:

CBS: January 9, 1959 through January 5, 1966 (144 episodes); Produced by: CBS Television; Executive Producer: Charles M. Warren; Producers: Vincent Fennelly, Bernard L. Kowalski, Bruce Geller, Endre Bohem, Ben Brady; Directors: Lee H. Katzin, Thomas Carr, Bernard Girard, Charles Warren, Tay Garnett, Ted Post, Earl Bellamy, Herschel Dougherty, Harry Harris, Don McDougall, Bernard McEveety, Andrew V. McLaglen; Music: Dimitri Tiomkin; Theme: Dimitri Tiomkin, Ned Washington; Theme Song Performer: Frankie Laine.

CAST:

Gil Favor	Eric Fleming
Rowdy Yates	Clint Eastwood

133

Don Durant and Mark Goddard

Clint Eastwood and Eric Fleming

Clint Eastwood as Rowdy
Yates in a scene from
Rawhide

Eric Fleming and guest star Jock Mahoney in *Rawhide*

Pete Nolan	. . . .	Sheb Wooley
Wishbone	. . . .	Paul Brinegar
Mushy	. . . .	James Murdock
Clay Forrester	. . . .	Charles Clay
Jim Quince	. . . .	Steve Raines

In the late 1950s, *Rawhide* had its debut. This landmark series had a deeper ring of authenticity than most shows which preceeded or followed it. And one of its stars, Clint Eastwood, was given a strong boost toward his stardom in films.

Rawhide depicted the story of a large cattle drive led by trail boss Gil Favor and his trail scout, Rowdy Yates, and the struggles and hardships they and their drovers had while attempting to deliver the herd from San Antonio to Sedalia, Kansas, in the 1860s. They encountered problems with Indians, cattle rustlers, deadly diseases, and unpredictable weather along the trail, and at various times the men themselves became quite irritated with one another. Their feuding added interest in the series.

Eric Fleming drowned September 28, 1966, while filming a movie on location in South America.

THE ALASKANS

Starring Roger Moore

CREDITS:

ABC: October 4, 1959 through September 25, 1960 (36 episodes); Produced by: Warner Brothers Television; Executive Producer: William T. Orr; Producers: Harry Tatelman, Boris Ingster; Directors: Richard Gordon, Charles Haas, Richard Sinclair, Jesse Hibbs, Robert Sparr, Jerry Leytes; Music: Mack David, Jerry Livingston, Paul Sawtell.

CAST:

Silky Harris	. . . .	Roger Moore
Rocky Shaw	. . . .	Dorothy Provine
Reno McKee	. . . .	Jeff York
Nifty Cronin	. . . .	Ray Danton
Soapy Smith	. . . .	John Dehner

The Alaskans was a Western adventure series set in 1898 in the frozen timberlands of Eagle City, Alaska.

Roger Moore

Logo for *The Alaskans*

135

Dorothy Provine, Roger Moore and Jeff York in *The Alaskans*

Three protagonists: Silky Harris, a smooth fast-talker; Reno McKee, a rugged hulking cowhand; and Rocky Shaw, a beautiful saloon singer, teamed up seeking to get rich quick in the last great Klondike Gold Rush. Rocky spent most of her time entertaining in the dance halls in Skagway and Dawson, while Harris and McKee were trying to figure out a way to mine gold that was buried deep in snow following an avalanche. Harris and McKee ran into many bushwackers along the trail in their search for the gold. Two such varmints were scoundrel Nifty Cronin and wheeler-dealer Soapy Smith. The former was a saloon owner who would help himself at another's expense and was not above having someone else do his dirty work. The latter would swindle, cheat, steal, or murder to get what he wanted. These two shifty characters and other evildoers plus a vast array of weekly challenges confronted the trio in their quest for gold.

THE REBEL

Starring Nick Adams

CREDITS:

ABC: October 4, 1959 through September 24, 1961 (76 episodes); Produced by: Goodson–Todman Produc-

tions; Executive Producer: Andrew J. Fenady; Director: Irvin Kershner; Creators: Andrew J. Fenady, Nick Adams; Music: Andrew Markowitz, Andrew J. Fenady; Theme Song Performer: Johnny Cash.

CAST:

Johnny Yuma . . . . Nick Adams

The Rebel told the story of Johnny Yuma, a bitter young ex-Confederate soldier of the post-Civil War era, searching for inner peace, who roamed through the untamed West during the 1860s still wearing parts of his Rebel uniform.

Yuma traveled around from town to town keeping a journal while getting involved with other people's problems. He continued to search for a place in life with his own personal brand of law, and sometimes his sawed-off double-barreled shotgun had to back it up.

This somewhat cerebral Western series differed a bit from the others of the era in that it dealt not only with the expected shoot-'em-up aspects of the genre but also with assorted moral issues.

The theme song of *The Rebel* was to have been performed by Elvis Presley, a close friend of title-star Nick Adams, at the time a teen idol, but the producer didn't approve it and used Johnny Cash instead.

Nick Adams committed suicide February 7, 1968.

Photo: Courtesy of TV Guide

136

Nick Adams in *The Rebel*

LARAMIE

Starring John Smith and Robert Fuller

CREDITS:

NBC: September 15, 1959 through September 17, 1963 (124 episodes); Produced by: Revue Productions; Producers: Don Williams, John Champion, Richard Lewis; Directors: Alvin Ganzer, Douglas Heyes, Joe Kane, Lesley Selander, Tay Garnett, Earl Bellamy; Music: Hans Salter, Richard Sendry; Theme: Cyril Mockridge.

CAST:

Slim Sherman	. . . .	John Smith
Jess Harper	. . . .	Robert Fuller

John Smith as Slim Sherman in *Laramie*

Robert Fuller and John Smith in a scene from *Laramie*

Robert Fuller in *Laramie*

Jonesy	Hoagy Carmichael
Andy Sherman	Robert Crawford, Jr.
Daisy Cooper	Spring Byington
Mike Williams	Dennis Holmes
Sheriff Mort Corey	Stuart Randall

Laramie was about the trials and tribulations of Slim Sherman and his younger brother Andy, left by themselves to run the Sherman ranch in Laramie, Wyoming, during the 1880s. Their father had been killed in a gunfight by a land pirate, leaving them in a difficult position with the ranch and barely able to survive. Fortunately, Slim is offered a contract from the government to use the ranch as a relay station for the Great Overland Mail Stage Lines.

The show's premise was established in *Laramie's* first episode, "The Drifter." Jess Harper, who was lightning fast with a gun, rode onto the Sherman ranch assisting Slim in a gunfight with outlaws. Slim was grateful for the help and asked Harper to stay on to help run the relay station. Harper's fast gun came in handy more times than once while protecting this swing station. The Sherman ranch, which also had a handyman named Jonesy and a housekeeper Daisy Cooper, saw its share of desperadoes passing through Laramie on a weekly basis.

The first 93 episodes were filmed in black and white; the next 31 in color.

Hoagy Carmichael died December 15, 1981.
Spring Byington died September 7, 1991.

RIVERBOAT

Starring Darren McGavin and
Burt Reynolds

CREDITS:

NBC: September 1, 1959 through January 16, 1961 (44 episodes); Produced by: Revue Productions; Producers: Jules Bricken, Richard Lewis, Richard Bartlett; Theme: Elmer Bernstein, Richard Sendry, Leo Shuken.

CAST:

Grey Holden	Darren McGavin
Ben Frazer	Burt Reynolds
Bill Blake	Noah Beery, Jr.
Travis	William D. Gordon

Riverboat plied the television waters for two seasons, a Western adventure series set along the routes of the Mississippi and Missouri Rivers during the 1840s. Grey Holden, captain of the riverboat *Enterprise*, wins the one-hundred-foot-long stern-wheeler in a poker game.

Darren McGavin

He puts the paddle wheeler to work carrying freight and passengers, determined to make it a profitable business. Ben Frazer played by Burt Reynolds in his first television starring role before spending time on the prairie in a recurring part on *Gunsmoke* for several seasons, is the pilot of the *Enterprise* and knows the Mississippi as well as any man and better than most.

Frazer was written out of the series midway through the first season and replaced later by a new pilot, Bill Blake, who bought 49 percent of the *Enterprise*, to provide Holden with more time for romantic entanglements with the ladies.

Professional con men, bushwackers, and beautiful ladies generated plenty of action in the show as they plotted and schemed their way along the river.

BLACK SADDLE

Starring Peter Breck

CREDITS:

NBC: January 19, 1959 through September 5, 1959; ABC: October 2, 1959 through September 30, 1960 (44 episodes); Produced by: Four Star Productions; Producers: Hal Hudson, Anthony Ellis; Creators: Hal Hudson, John McGreevey; Directors: John English, William F. Claxton, Gerd Oswald, David Lowell Rich;

Peter Breck in *Black Saddle*

Music: Jerry Goldsmith, Arthur Morton; Theme: Jerry Goldsmith, J. Michael Hannigan, Arthur Morton.

CAST:

Clay Culhane	Peter Breck
Marshal Gib Scott	Russell Johnson
Nora Travers	Anna-Lisa
Kelly, the bartender	Ken Patterson

Westerns were increasingly popular in the late 1950s. Among those was *Black Saddle*, bearing an unusual title for a television series. The setting was Latigo, New Mexico, during the 1860s, a time when a few gunslingers were trying to turn over a new leaf, as was Clay Culhane, an ex-gunfighter who had lost all his brothers in gunfights. Consequently, he decided to look to other solutions in settling his problems. Culhane became a lawyer and hung out his shingle in Latigo; however, few were convinced that he had given up his gunslinging days. U.S. Marshal Gib Scott (Russell Johnson, later the Professor on *Gilligan's Island*) kept a close eye on Culhane, and so did Nora Travers, who owned the Marathon Hotel, where Culhane's operations were based. Culhane traveled the West offering his assis-

Peter Breck as Clay Culhane

tance to citizens in their legal affairs, avoiding any violence if possible. He kept his law books in his saddlebags, thus explaining the title of this Western: *Black Saddle*.

HOTEL de PAREE

Starring Earl Holliman

CREDITS:

CBS: September 17, 1959 through September 5, 1960 (33 episodes); Produced by: CBS; Executive Producer: William Self; Producer: Stanley Rubin; Music: Van Alexander.

CAST:

Sundance	Earl Holliman
Annette Devereaux,	
hotel manager	Jeanette Nolan

Earl Holliman as Sundance

Monique Devereaux	Judi Meredith
Aaron Donager	Strother Martin

In the television Western series *Hotel de Paree*, an ex-gunslinger known as Sundance has returned to a town after serving a long prison term. The center of activity is the colorful Hotel de Paree, an establishment with a European flair, located in Georgetown, Colorado, during the 1870s, and run by Annette Devereaux and her pretty niece Monique. Sundance had accidently killed a man at the hotel, and on his release from prison after seventeen years, he has come home to find the relatives of the man he killed owning the Hotel de Paree. Annette and Monique were being harassed by gunmen, drunken cowhands, and other townsfolk. However, Sundance comes to their rescue. Chivalrous and deadly with his gun, he uses highly polished silver discs on his hatband either to blind his opponents or, sometimes in trouble, to signal help. Sundance's two friends were old codger Aaron Donager and faithful dog Useless.

Strother Martin died August 1, 1980.

SHOTGUN SLADE

Starring Scott Brady

CREDITS:

Syndicated: November 1959 through 1962 (78 episodes); Produced by: Revue Productions; Executive Producer: Nat Holt; Producer: Frank Gruber; Director: Sidney Salkow; Music: Stanley Wilson; Theme Song Performer: Monica Lewis.

CAST:

Shotgun Slade	Scott Brady
Alice Barton	Marie Windsor
Monica	Monica Lewis

Shotgun Slade was a double-barreled action Western but unfortunately a series that got lost in the West. Few people remember this late fifties-early sixties series; nevertheless, it was a good show. Some of the television stations claimed the show had violence too strong for their audience, so *Slade* took the leftovers, the afternoons or late-night slots, instead of prime time.

Slade was a detective on horseback who attempted

Scott Brady as Shotgun Slade

to tame the West and its wildest bad men during the 1880s. He carried a unique, custom-made, two-in-one double-barreled shotgun that he preferred instead of a normal six-gun. Slade hired out his services to banks, insurance companies, Wells Fargo, and others needing protection for one reason or another and found plenty of action in every episode. Slade's romantic interest in the show was Monica, and his close friend was Alice Barton who ran the saloon in town.

Scott Brady died April 17, 1985.

THE MAN FROM BLACKHAWK

Starring Robert Rockwell

CREDITS:

ABC: October 9, 1959 through September 24, 1960 (23 episodes); Produced by: Screen Gems/Stuart-Oliver Productions; Producer: Herb Meadow; Director: John Peyser.

CAST:

Sam Logan . . . . Robert Rockwell

The Man From Blackhawk was a rather violent series about rugged Sam Logan, who worked as a special investigator for the Blackhawk Insurance Company based in Chicago during the 1870s. He followed up cases involving fake insurance claims and other criminal schemes to defraud the company. Looking the very image of a greenhorn, Logan traveled through the Western Frontier in a pin-striped business suit with a string tie while carrying his briefcase. Unlike other cowboys, he almost always arrived by stagecoach to investigate his cases and rarely on horseback.

Sam Logan was not a pushover by any means and seldom carried a gun for protection. With his powerful fists and fast reactions, he was capable of defending himself or anyone traveling with him. Everyone knew if they would dare to defraud Blackhawk they had best be prepared to meet Sam Logan in this Western with a decided twist.

Robert Rockwell and guest star Barbara Lawrence in a scene from *The Man From Blackhawk*

WICHITA TOWN

Starring Joel McCrea and Jody McCrea

CREDITS:

NBC: September 30, 1959 through September 23, 1960 (24 episodes); Produced by: Walter Mirisch Productions; Executive Producer: Frank Baur; Producer: Walter Mirisch; Music: Hans Salter.

CAST:

Marshal Mike Dunbar	Joel McCrea
Ben Matheson	Jody McCrea
Rico Rodriguez	Carlos Romero

Movie veteran Joel McCrea starred in *Wichita Town*, based vaguely on his 1955 film *Wichita*. This was the only time McCrea ever agreed to do a television series, which costarred his real-life son Jody, who played one of his deputies.

The series told of the efforts of U.S. Marshal Mike Dunbar, the arm for law enforcement in Wichita, Kansas, during the 1870s. Dunbar had arrived in Wichita after ramroding a cattle drive and selected the town for his home. Accepting his newly appointed job as marshal of Wichita, Dunbar and his deputies, Ben Matheson and Rico Rodriquez, dealt with the many problems of cattle rustlers, roving gamblers, and violence in those turbulent times.

Joel McCrea died October 20, 1990.

William Bendix and Doug McClure

OVERLAND TRAIL

Starring William Bendix and Doug McClure

CREDITS:

NBC: February 7, 1960 through September 11, 1960 (17 episodes); Produced by: Revue Productions; Executive Producer: Nat Holt; Producer: Samuel A. Peeples; Director: Virgil W. Vogel; Music: Stanley Wilson.

CAST:

Frederick Thomas Kelly	William Bendix
Frank "Flip" Flippen	Doug McClure

Joel McCrea and Jody McCrea

Overland Trail was one of the first attempts to make a television series dealing with the operation of a stagecoach line. *Stagecoach West* and *Whiplash*, with similar story lines, met the same fate as *Overland Trail*. The Overland stage came to the end of the line after making only seventeen runs on NBC.

It followed the exploits of Frederick Thomas Kelly, the crusty superintendent of the Overland Stage Line, a new operation, and his sidekick, the Indian-raised Frank "Flip" Flippen, as they attempted to establish the first stage line between the Mississippi River and California in the 1860s. Kelly (played by burly William Bendix, who had gained radio and television immortality earlier in *The Life of Riley*) was a former Civil War engineer determined to open two thousand miles of wilderness with his new stagecoach route. Kelly and Flip (Doug McClure, who would later go on to star as Trampas on *The Virginian*) encountered the familiar perils that followed close behind stagecoaches, such as Indian attacks, holdups, bad varmints, and rotten weather, which proved all in a day's work for this rugged twosome. In the first episode, the outlaw Cole Younger was being transferred by the Overland stage to another territory for a trial. The stage stopped at a relay station only to find the notorious Belle Starr waiting to free Younger—unsuccessfully, of course.

Brian Keith and Brown

THE WESTERNER

Starring Brian Keith

CREDITS:

NBC: September 30, 1960 through December 30, 1960 (13 episodes); Produced by: Four Star Productions; Executive Producer: Hal Hudson; Producer: Sam Peckinpah; Creator: Sam Peckinpah; Directors: Sam Peckinpah, Bernard L. Kowalski, André De Toth, Elliot Silverstein; Music: Rudy Schrager, Joseph Mullendore.

CAST:

Dave Blassingame	Brian Keith
Burgundy Smith	John Dehner

Sam Peckinpah created, produced, and occasionally directed this short-lived series called *The Westerner*. By the time this one came out in the fall of 1960, Westerns were losing audiences to detective shows and comedy sitcoms. *The Westerner* only survived thirteen episodes before being canceled.

Brian Keith in *The Westerner*

Dave Blassingame was a drifter who roamed from town to town in the 1880s with his traveling companion, a dog named Brown. Blassingame seemed to be plagued by the lovable con man Burgundy Smith during his journeys. This was basically a show played for its humorous content. In one episode, Dave arrives in a small town and meets up with Burgundy. While they talk, Brown wanders into the general store and begins chasing a cat, causing a total disaster. The store owner gets the sheriff and asks Dave and Burgundy if they own the dog. Both deny that the dog belongs to them. The sheriff has each man call the dog to determine his master. Totally unexpectedly, Brown goes to Burgundy. Neither Dave nor Burgundy has money to pay the damages which becomes another part of the story.

John Dehner died February 4, 1992.

TATE

Starring David McLean

CREDITS:

NBC: June 8, 1960 through September 28, 1960 (13 episodes); Produced by: Roncom Video Films Production; Executive Producer: Alan Cooperman; Producer: Shelly Hull; Director: Richard Whorf; Created by: Harry Julian Fink.

CAST:

Tate . . . . David McLean
Jessica Jackson . . . . Patricia Breslin

Tate, a 1960 summer replacement series on NBC, offered a "different" Western character. This television Western was loaded with action and color. Unfortunately, it was canceled without getting deserved recognition.

Tate was a one-armed, Bible-quoting ex-gunfighter who fought on the side of the law in the 1870s. During the Civil War, Tate's left arm had been all but blown from his shoulder in the battle at Vicksburg. His shattered limb was bound in a black rawhide-leather casing, which ran all the way from his fingertips to above the elbow. Tate's wife and child had been killed during the war, and when he returned home he learned that they had already been buried.

With no other choice, he became a wandering fast-

gun-for-hire on the frontier. Vainly, he searched for something to relieve the pain of his family's death. Another man might have chosen a lawless path following such an ordeal, but Tate couldn't. His values in life remained the same, but Tate was not one to mess around with. His handicap did not make him less than an expert with a gun, and he was constantly being challenged to prove his past reputation as a gunfighter. However, when the enemy called on him, they didn't call again.

Tate is best remembered by trivia buffs for two guest appearances by an up-and-coming Robert Redford.

David McLean

Ralph Taeger as Mike Halliday

This short-lived turn-of-the-century television Western only survived eighteen episodes on NBC. The setting was Skagway, Alaska, in 1897, and it was based on Pierre Benton's gold-rush novel *The Klondike Fever*.

It was about the exploits of an adventurer, Mike Halliday, in his search for gold in the dangerous Ice Palace of the Northland. In Skagway, Halliday had his share of trouble with Jeff Durain, a gambler who owned the Golden Nugget, where the miners regularly lost their dollars on games of chance. The scoundrel Durain was always scheming to make a fast buck, while Mike tried to reveal his conniving plans before they happened. Kathy O'Hara ran the only honest hotel in town and often helped Mike foil Durain. Kathy was in love with Mike, but he was too busy trying to strike it rich to notice, although he usually found time to visit the beautiful buxom blond dance-hall girl Goldie, who was Jeff Durain's greedy assistant.

The most unusual thing about the series was that the week after its demise, Taeger and Coburn took their characters (under other names) from north of the border to south of the border fifty years hence in the even shorter-lived adventure series *Acapulco*.

Mari Blanchard died May 10, 1970.

Joi Lansing died August 7, 1972.

KLONDIKE

Starring Ralph Taeger

CREDITS:

NBC: October 10, 1960 through February 13, 1961 (18 episodes); Produced by: ZIV-United Artists Television; Executive Producer: William Conrad; Directors: Sam Peckinpah, William Conrad; Music: Vic Mizzy.

CAST:

Mike Halliday	Ralph Taeger
Kathy O'Hara	Mari Blanchard
Jeff Durain	James Coburn
Goldie	Joi Lansing
Uncle Jonah	J. Pat O'Malley

STAGECOACH WEST

Starring Wayne Rogers and Robert Bray

CREDITS:

ABC: October 4, 1960 through September 26, 1961 (26 episodes); Produced by: Four Star Productions; Producer: Vincent M. Fennelly; Directors: Thomas Carr, Harry Harris, Don McDougall; Music: Jerry Fielding, Herschel Burke Gilbert.

CAST:

Luke Perry	Wayne Rogers
Simon Kane	Robert Bray
David Kane	Richard Eyer

Stagecoach West rolled into ABC prime time on Tuesday nights in 1960. It was a Western adventure series concerning the Timberland Stage Line making runs from Tipton, Missouri, to San Francisco during the 1860s.

The line was run by Luke Perry and Simon Kane,

Wayne Rogers (left), Robert Bray, and Richard Eyer in *Stagecoach West*

Robert Bray (left), Richard Eyer, and Wayne Rogers

both excellent and experienced drivers, and they encountered all kinds of adventures during their trips, including holdups, robberies, Indian attacks, and bad weather conditions. The passengers they carried and the people they met en route provided the stories for the series. Luke and Simon were a great team together in protecting their passengers and valuable shipments.

After a single season, however, *Stagecoach West* came to the end of the trail, put out of business probably by the encroaching railroad system.

Robert Bray died March 7, 1983.

THE TALL MAN

Starring Barry Sullivan and Clu Gulager

CREDITS:

NBC: September 10, 1960 through September 1, 1962 (75 episodes); Produced by: Revue Productions; Executive Producers: Nat Holt, Edward J. Montagne; Producers: Samuel A. Peeples, Frank Price; Creator: Samuel A. Peeples; Directors: Herschel Daugherty, Lesley Selander; Music: Juan Esquivel.

CAST:

Sheriff Pat Garrett	Barry Sullivan
William "Billy the Kid" Bonney . . .	Clu Gulager

The Tall Man told fancifully about the life and times of Sheriff Pat Garrett and his relationship with Billy the Kid. In Lincoln County, New Mexico, during the 1870s, William H. Bonney, better known as Billy the Kid, a young gunslinger, had a penchant for getting in trouble with the law. Bonney, in fact, was depicted merely as a misguided young man, not a sadistic killer. Despite the fact they were on opposite sides, Pat Garrett and Billy Bonney were close friends. Pat looked upon Billy as a younger brother or son but somehow knew that someday they would be forced to a showdown. Pat regarded a gun as a way of survival when there was no alternative. Billy, though, saw his gun as the great equalizer.

Barry Sullivan as Sheriff Pat Garrett

Clu Gulager as Billy the Kid

His unlawful activities kept bringing him and Pat closer to the day of reckoning. Garrett's credo, "My business is the law and I mean to mind it," showed that the confrontation between the two men was inevitable. In actuality, Pat Garrett did eventually shoot down Billy in a gunfight, but the killing was never shown in the series.

THE OUTLAWS

Starring Barton MacLane

CREDITS:

NBC: September 29, 1960 through September 13, 1962 (50 episodes); Produced by: Revlon–Revue Productions; Executive Producer: Frank Telford; Producer: Joseph Dackow; Music: Hugo Friedhofer.

CAST:

Marshal Frank Caine . . . . Barton MacLane
Deputy Chalk Breeson . . . . . Bruce Yarnell

Barton Maclane

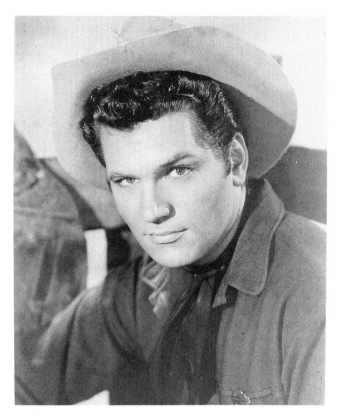

Bruce Yarnell in *The Outlaws*

Deputy Heck Martin . . . . Jock Gaynor
Deputy Will Foreman . . . . . . Don Collier
Slim . . . . Slim Pickens
Constance Masters . . . . Judy Lewis

The Outlaws told the story of United States Marshal Frank Caine and his deputies enforcing law and order in Stillwater, Oklahoma, during the 1890s. They had run-ins with infamous outlaws such as the Dalton and the Jennings gangs, some of the leading desperadoes of the West. In the first season, the events were seen through the eyes of the hunted; after that through those of the marshal.

The danger in dealing with vicious outlaw gangs of this sort was that the lawmen were usually outnumbered and going against men who had nothing to lose. Unless the lawmen formed a posse and had superior planning skills and dedication by marshals like Frank Caine, they could be chasing their last bad man.

After the first season of *The Outlaws*, Marshal Caine left the show, promoting Deputy Will Foreman to full marshal of Stillwater. Another new citizen showed up in town, Slim, played by character actor Slim Pickens.

Barton MacLane died January 1, 1969.
Slim Pickens died December 8, 1983.

WHISPERING SMITH

Starring Audie Murphy

CREDITS:

NBC: May 8, 1961 through September 18, 1961 (25 episodes); Produced by: Revue Productions; Executive Producer: Richard Lewis; Producers: Herbert Coleman, Willard Willingham; Music: Richard Shores, Leo Shuken.

CAST:

Tom "Whispering" Smith . . . . . Audie Murphy
George Romack . . . . Guy Mitchell
Chief John Richards . . . . . Sam Buffington

Guy Mitchell (left) and Audie Murphy

The series *Whispering Smith*, which was based on the 1948 Alan Ladd movie, seemed to be doomed from the very beginning. The problem-plagued show was movie star Audie Murphy's only attempt to do a television Western. Very unhappy about the way the show's production was being handled, he complained about the scripts, the directors, and the crew. Production had to be held up for several weeks when Murphy's costar, pop singer-turned-actor Guy Mitchell, fell from a horse, breaking his arm. No sooner did the show resume then Sam Buffington, one of the cast members, committed suicide and had to be replaced. Bad news kept coming after the first episode was aired. The Senate Juvenile Delinquency committee filed charges against the network, claiming the show was too violent. *Whispering Smith* had begun filming in 1959, but with the show's history of problems in production it would be 1961 before the series began airing, and then it ran only briefly.

Whispering Smith was a detective-type Western which focused on an investigator for the Denver railroad during the 1870s, based on official files of the Denver police department. The cases were handled by Tom "Whispering" Smith and his partner George Romack, protecting the railroad from fraud, robberies and murder, and using methods of tracing and apprehending outlaws standard in modern criminology.

The most decorated soldier in U.S. history, Audie Murphy died in a plane crash near Roanoke, Virginia, on May 28, 1971. He was buried in Arlington National Cemetery with full military honors.

GUNSLINGER

Starring Tony Young

Tony Young as Cord in *Gunslinger*

CREDITS:

CBS: February 9, 1961 through September 14, 1961 (12 episodes); Produced by: CBS; Executive Producer: Charles Marquis Warren; Creator: Charles Marquis Warren; Theme: Dimitri Tiomkin.

CAST:

Cord . . . . Tony Young
Capt. Zachary Wingate . . . . Preston Foster
Amber Hollister . . . . Midge Ware
Pico McGuire . . . . Charles Gray
Billy Urchin . . . . Dee Pollock
Sergeant Major Murdock . . . . John Pickard

In this short-lived hour-long television Western, a man known only as Cord became an undercover agent for Capt. Zachary Wingate, commandant of the cavalry at Fort Scott in Los Flores, New Mexico, during the 1860s. An expert with a six-gun, Cord posed as a gunslinger to apprehend criminals wanted by the United States Army and to work on undercover assignments. He often disagreed with Capt. Wingate as to how the criminals should be apprehended, and used his own method when the bad guys did not heed to his calling. That usually meant with the action of his Colt .45. His friends Pico and Billy were trusted enough by Capt. Wingate to accompany Cord on his secret missions. Cord's romantic interest was the beautiful Amber

Hollister, who ran the general store at Fort Scott. He could always count on her enchanting smile when he returned from his journeys.

THE VIRGINIAN

Starring James Drury

CREDITS:

NBC: September 16, 1962 through September 9, 1970 (225 episodes); Produced by: Revue Productions; Executive Producers: Leslie Stevens, Herbert Hirschman, Norman MacDonnell; Producers: Roy Huggins, Frank Price, James Duff, Richard Irving, James McAdams, Jules Schermer; Directors: Roy Huggins, Charles Dubin, Leo Penn, Bernard Girard, Don Weis, Thomas Carr, Herschel Daugherty, Gene Coon; Music: Max Steiner, Leonard Rosenman, Hans Salter, Leo Shuken; Theme: Percy Faith.

CAST:

The Virginian	James Drury
Judge Henry Garth (first ranch owner)	Lee J. Cobb
John Grainger (second ranch owner)	Charles Bickford
Clay Grainger (third ranch owner)	John McIntire
Trampas	Doug McClure
Betsy Garth	Roberta Shore
Randy Garth	Randy Boone
Deputy Emmett Ryker	Clu Gulager
Steve Hill	Gary Clarke
Molly Wood	Pippa Scott

James Drury

Television's first ninety-minute adult Western drama was *The Virginian*, based on Owen Wister's 1902 novel of the same name. Several motion pictures have been made under the title, *The Virginian*, perhaps the most famous with Gary Cooper in 1929 and Joel McCrea in 1946. James Drury was chosen to star initially in the television series in 1958. However, *The Virginian's* first showing on the small screen was unsuccessful. The character rode into town dressed in a Western garb with lace cuffs, shiny boots and skintight pants. The Western fans were not interested in this cowboy regardless of who he was. In 1962, Drury returned to the role again wearing a different outfit that captured the television audience. The show was an overnight hit and lasted nearly eight years.

The plot concerned a mysterious stranger who never revealed his identity and was known only as the Virginian. No one knew his origin, only that he was fast with a gun and short on words.

He became foreman of the Shiloh ranch in Medicine Bow, Wyoming, in the 1880s and was loyal to the family he worked for: Judge Henry Garth and his daughter Betsy and his son Randy. Trampas was the rowdy and irresponsible ranch hand who often found it difficult to follow orders, and Deputy Emmett Ryker enforced the law in the Wyoming Territory.

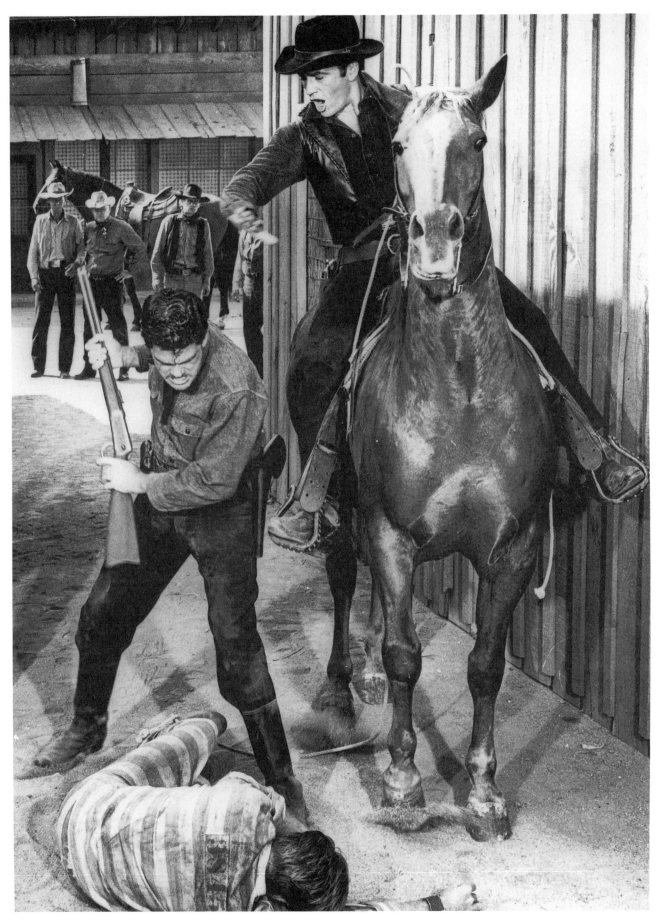

James Drury as The Virginian

Lee J. Cobb in *The Virginian*

The Men From Shiloh lasted twenty-four episodes.
Lee J. Cobb died February 11, 1976.
Charles Bickford died November 9, 1967.
John McIntire died January 30, 1991.

James Drury and guest star Kathleen Crowley in a scene from *The Virginian*

The Virginian attracted many top-name performers passing through Medicine Bow, such as Bette Davis, Joan Crawford, Telly Savalas, Charles Bronson, Lee Marvin, Broderick Crawford, and Robert Redford. The Virginian was a tough hombre when he had to be, but on the other hand, he was gentle and caring. He was honest and fair in making a judgment on an issue and more than once risked his life to help his fellow man.

In fall 1970, the show was revamped and called *The Men From Shiloh*, with James Drury still playing the Virginian and Doug McClure continuing as Trampas. Lee Majors joined them as Tate, a new hand, as did Stewart Granger, as the new owner of the Shiloh ranch.

EMPIRE

Starring Richard Egan

CREDITS:

NBC: September 25, 1962 through September 17, 1963 (32 episodes); Produced by: Screen Gems; Executive Producer: Frank Parson; Producer: William Sackheim; Music: Johnny Green.

CAST:

Jim Redigo	Richard Egan
Lucia Garrett	Anne Seymour
Connie Garrett	Terry Moore
Tal Garrett	Ryan O'Neal

Richard Egan

including his superiors, hired hands, or any outside advisers. Redigo was always on target with decisions, and he rode for the brand.

Empire may not have been a shoot-'em-up type Western with six-guns blazing, but there was plenty of familiar action with shady characters, including cattle rustlers, shifty politicians, and other ornery critters, passing through each episode. A spin-off series, *Redigo*, with Richard Egan and a whole new cast, began on NBC the week after *Empire* left, and ran for 15 episodes through the end of 1963.

Richard Egan died July 20, 1987.

Paul Moreno . . . . Charles Bronson
Chuck . . . . Warren Vanders

Empire was different from other television Westerns even though it dealt with the similar story line of the problems occurring on a sprawling half-million-acre ranch. *Empire* was a contemporary Western, a soap-opera-in-buckskins forerunner of modern-day Westerns such as *Dallas* and *Dynasty*.

The lead character was Jim Redigo, the no-nonsense foreman of the wealthy Garrett family's multimillion-dollar spread in Santa Fe. Redigo was one tough character who refused to compromise with anyone

Richard Egan as Jim Redigo

153

Jack Lord

STONEY BURKE

Starring Jack Lord

CREDITS:

ABC: October 1, 1962 through September 2, 1963 (32 episodes); Produced by: Daystar Productions, United Artists Television; Producer: Leslie Stevens; Director: Leslie Stevens; Music: Dominic Frontiere.

CAST:

Stoney Burke	Jack Lord
E. J. Stocker	Bruce Dern
Wes Painter	Warren Oates
Cody Bristal	Robert Dowdell
Red	Bill Hart

Stoney Burke was a modern-day Western (like *Wide Country* the same season) about cowboys and rodeos

but never seemed to catch on with the viewers. Somehow television shows about rodeos and stage lines appealed only to a limited audience.

This series depicted the rugged life of rodeo champion rider Stoney Burke, who traveled the circuits trying to win the Golden Buckle Award, a trophy given only to the world's best saddle-bronc riders. Burke and pals toured from rodeo to rodeo with a dream he would find the right saddle bronc to win the award, usually facing his share of bull-headed cowboys with their own crooked schemes that caused him considerable setbacks. Unfortunately, the single-season series was canceled before Stoney Burke ever won his Golden Buckle Award.

Jack Lord would go on, of course, to earn lots of money later as the star of *Hawaii Five-O*. Up-and-coming Bruce Dern and Warren Oates would become cult figures on the big screen in Westerns by Sam Peckinpah, Burt Kennedy, and others.

Warren Oates died April 3, 1982.

Jack Lord as Stoney Burke

154

THE DAKOTAS

Starring Larry Ward

CREDITS:

ABC: January 7, 1963 through September 9, 1963 (19 episodes); Produced by: Warner Brothers Television;

Executive Producer: William T. Orr; Producers: Anthony Spinner, Jerome Schermer; Directors: Robert Totten, Richard Sarafian, Charles Rondeau, Richard Bare, Stuart Heisler; Music: Frank Perkins, Warren Barker.

CAST:

Marshal Frank Regan	Larry Ward
Deputy Del Stark	Chad Everett
Deputy J. D. Smith	Jack Elam
Deputy Vance Porter	Michael Greene

One of the last hour-long television Westerns produced by Warner Brothers was *The Dakotas*, set in the post-Civil War period. This spin-off, from an episode of *Cheyenne* called "A Man Called Regan," followed Marshal Frank Regan and his three deputies: J.D.

Larry Ward in *The Dakotas*

Chad Everett

Smith, Del Stark, and Vance Porter, who attempted to keep law and order in the Black Hills of Dakota Territory. The four dealt with much violence tracking down wanted criminals. Regan was a dedicated lawman who would go to any extreme to uphold the law.

The show's demise came after an episode showing Deputy Smith chasing an outlaw into a church and killing him there. This scene caused a great deal of controversy; the mail poured in, and ABC had no choice but to cancel the show. (The producers, according to one story consultant, also had gotten into hot water when MGM accused Warners of having appropriated elements for the series from its film *Bad Day at Black Rock*.)

Larry Ward died on February 16, 1983.

Michael Greene, Larry Ward, Jack Elam and Chad Everett

Fess Parker as *Daniel Boone*

DANIEL BOONE

Starring Fess Parker

CREDITS:

NBC: September 24, 1964 through September 10, 1970 (165 episodes); Produced by: 20th Century-Fox Television, Arcola-Fespar Productions; Executive Produc-

Fess Parker and Patricia Blair

158

ers: Aaron Spelling, Aaron Rosenberg; Producers: Joseph Silver, George Sherman, Barney Rosenzweig; Directors: Earl Bellamy, William Witney, Fess Parker, John Newland, Barry Shear, Nathan Juran, George Marshall, Gerd Oswald; Music: Alexander Courage, Leith Stevens, Harry Sukman, Fred Steiner, Lyn Murray, Irving Getz; Theme Song Performer: The Imperials Quartet.

CAST:

Daniel Boone	Fess Parker
Rebecca Boone	Patricia Blair
Jemima Boone	Veronica Cartwright
Israel Boone	Darby Hinton
Yadkin	Albert Salmi
Mingo	Ed Ames
Cincinnatus	Dallas McKennon
Josh Clements	Jimmy Dean
Gabe Cooper	Roosevelt Grier

Daniel Boone was another successful Western adventure series starring Fess Parker, following his star-making *Davy Crockett*. There was one thing different in Parker's *Daniel Boone* series, however; it was not produced by Disney, which passed on a Boone series, leaving Parker, under contract to Disney for television as well as movies, free to go elsewhere. Shortly afterwards Parker began his adventures as *Daniel Boone* on NBC. (Actually, Disney did do a short-lived, four-episode Daniel Boone series in 1960–61 with Dewey Martin.)

Daniel Boone was one of America's most colorful figures as a legendary frontiersman, pioneer, and explorer during the latter half of the eighteenth century. Boone's expeditions took him to the untamed wilderness of many meadowlands before settling in Boonesborough Kentucky. Never satisfied to stay in one place for a long period of time, Boone craved excitement and adventure while exploring the unknown with his handmade Kentucky long rifle. He lived with his wife Rebecca, his young son Israel, and a daughter Jemima, and was surrounded by many loyal friends during his adventures: Yadkin, his sidekick; Mingo, an Oxford-educated Cherokee Indian; and Cincinnatus, a cranky old barkeeper.

Albert Salmi committed suicide on April 22, 1989, after killing his wife.

THE WILD, WILD WEST

Starring Robert Conrad and Ross Martin

CREDITS:

CBS: September 17, 1965 through September 19, 1969 (104 episodes); Produced by: CBS; Executive Producers: Philip Leacock, Michael Garrison; Producers: Richard Landau, John Mantley, Collier Young, Leonard Katzman, Bruce Lansbury, Gene L. Coon, Fred Freid-

Ross Martin and Robert Conrad

Robert Conrad as James West and Ross Martin as Artemus Gordon

berger; Directors: William Witney, Don Taylor, Alvin Ganzer, Lee H. Katzin, Alan Copeland; Music: Richard Shores, Richard Markowitz, Morton Stevens.

CAST:

James T. West	Robert Conrad
Artemus Gordon	Ross Martin

The Wild, Wild West, one of television's most popular and imaginative Westerns, was forced off the air after a four-year run on CBS because Congress and government officials believed it to be too violent.

The show was set during the 1870s, when lawless guns had taken over most of the West. Undercover agents, suave James T. West and Artemus Gordon, a master of disguise, worked for President Ulysses S. Grant as his Secret Service investigators. Their missions took them on a series of unusual adventures that put them up against villains who were not your ordinary cowboys in familiar situations. These characters were walking zombies, electric toy soldiers, even megalomaniacal dwarfs. West and Gordon traveled on their assignments in a special railroad car, where their disguises, explosives, and other scientific weapons were used to rid the territory of criminals. The consumate showman Artemus Gordon was a genius at disguising himself as any character and acted as the perfect foil to the athletic Jim West. Both men performed their own stunts.

Robert Conrad in *The Wild, Wild West*

Ross Martin and Robert Conrad in *The Wild, Wild West*

161

Robert Conrad in a
scene from *The Wild,
Wild West*

Robert Conrad as Jim West caught in another captured moment in *The Wild, Wild West*.

162

Eighteen years after the series' demise, the two were called out of retirement to reprise their crimefighting roles in two television movies, which got the kind of audience reception to warrant a new series that might have been had not Ross Martin died.

Ross Martin died July 3, 1981.

THE LONER

Starring Lloyd Bridges

CREDITS:

CBS: September 18, 1965 through April 30, 1966 (26 episodes); Produced by: 20th Century-Fox Television/Greenway Productions; Executive Producer: William Dozier; Producers: Andy White, Bruce Lansbury; Director: Alex March; Creator: Rod Serling; Music: Jerry Goldsmith, Nelson Riddle, Lalo Schifrin.

CAST:

William Colton . . . . Lloyd Bridges

The Loner was a short-lived series created by Rod Serling, of *The Twilight Zone*. It was reported that Lloyd Bridges, the star of *The Loner*, became unhappy about the violence and number of gunfights written into the show. Although the show was critically acclaimed, the violence was perhaps the reason for its short run.

The Loner was the story of William Colton, a disillusioned Union cavalry officer during the post-Civil War period. Disenchanted with the war, Colton resigned his commission, determined to clear the cannon smoke from his eyes, free the noise from his ears, and

Lloyd Bridges in *The Loner*

look for a more meaningful life. Heading West, he wandered the frontier from town to town on a beautiful coal-black horse finding anything but peace. It was still one gunfight after another wherever he roamed. When the show was canceled, there was still noise on CBS in this thirty-minute time slot from a new game show.

Lloyd Bridges

Barbara Stanwyck

THE BIG VALLEY

Starring Barbara Stanwyck

CREDITS:

ABC: September 12, 1965 through May 19, 1969 (112 episodes); Produced by: Four Star Productions; Executive Producers: Jules Levy, Arthur Gardner, Arnold Laven; Producer: Lou Morheim; Directors: Virgil W.

(From left) Richard Long, Lee Majors, Linda Evans, Barbara Stanwyck, and Peter Breck

Photo by: Gene Trindl

Linda Evans as Audra

Vogel, Don Taylor, Bernard McEveety, Ida Lupino, Arthur Nadel, Charles Dubin, Lawrence Dobkin, Michael Ritchie; Music: Joseph Mullendore, Elmer Bernstein; Theme: George Dunning.

CAST:

Victoria Barkley	Barbara Stanwyck
Jarrod	Richard Long
Nick	Peter Breck
Audra	Linda Evans
Heath	Lee Majors
Silas, the servant	Napoleon Whiting
Eugene	Charles Briles

The Big Valley was one of television's most popular Westerns during the 1960s when the cowboys began to fade from the screen. It was also the first Western carried by a actress, and still one of the only ones. The

Barbara Stanwyck as Victoria Barkley

setting for *The Big Valley* was in California's San Joaquin Valley in 1878.

It was the story of Victoria Barkley, a strong-willed, determined matriarch and owner of a thirty thousand-acre cattle ranch. Her family included Jarrod, an attorney in Stockton; Nick, the two-fisted ranch foreman; Heath, an illegitimate son of Victoria's deceased husband Tom; and Audra, a very beautiful young lady waiting for the right man to capture her heart. (Early in the series there was another son, shy and sensitive Eugene, but he was dropped.) Together the Barkleys fought drought, cattle rustlers, trespassers, kidnappers, and escaped killers. The rugged clan was faced with problems of violence and lawlessness every week but somehow managed to find the strength through family unity to persevere.

Barbara Stanwyck died January 20, 1990.

Richard Long died December 12, 1974.

F TROOP

Starring Forrest Tucker, Ken Berry, and Larry Storch

CREDITS:

ABC: September 14, 1965 through September 7, 1967 (65 episodes); Produced by: Warner Brothers Television; Executive Producers: William T. Orr, Hy Averback; Producer: Herm Saunders; Directors: Hal March, Gene Reynolds, David Alexander, Charles Rondeau, Leslie Goodwins, Seymour Robbie; Music: Richard

Forrest Tucker and Larry Storch

Larry Storch as Corporal Agarn

LaSalle, Frank Comstock, William Lava; Theme: William Lava, Irving Taylor.

CAST:

Sgt. Morgan O'Rourke	Forrest Tucker
Capt. Wilton Parmenter	Ken Berry
Cpl. Randolph Agarn	Larry Storch
Wrangler Jane	Melody Patterson
Trooper Duffy	Bob Steele
Bugler Dobbs	James Hampton
Trooper Vanderbilt	Joe Brooks
Bald Eagle	Don Rickles
Roaring Chicken	Edward Everett Horton

F Troop was a comedy Western series about the misadventures of incompetent but memorable cavalry goof-ups who were not your ordinary heroes of the U.S. Army. The setting was Fort Courage, Kansas, in the post-Civil War period of 1866. These troopers were more interested in selling Indian trinkets than in fighting the Indians who made them. Sergeant O'Rourke, played by Forrest Tucker, had more than a passing interest in the nearby saloon; he was the owner of the establishment. In fact, these stalwart defenders of the American way of life had gone so far as to make a secret treaty with the Hekawi Indians and were coexisting with them in a prosperous business relationship.

Included in this classic roster of goofballs and misfits were Corporal Agarn, the post scrounger; Private Vanderbilt, a nearsighted tower lookout; Hannibal Dobbs, a bungling bugler, who couldn't blow three notes in tune; and finally, curvy, tight-jeaned Wrangler

Ken Berry and Melody Patterson

168

Jane, proprietor of the fort's general store, who was more interested in wrangling a marriage out of the post captain than in horses for the army. Capt. Wilton Parmenter went from a private in charge of the officer's laundry to the Fort's company commander in a rather unique manner. While doing the laundry one day, an excess of pollen caused him to sneeze and blurt out what sounded like "CHARGE!" Troopers went into action immediately, bringing about a stunning Union victory over the Confederates.

Forrest Tucker died October 26, 1986.

BRANDED

Starring Chuck Connors

CREDITS:

NBC: January 24, 1965 through September 4, 1966 (48 episodes); Produced by: Goodson-Todman Productions; Executive Producer: Andrew J. Fenady; Producer: Cecil Barker; Creator: Larry Cohen; Directors: William Witney, Joseph H. Lewis, Lee H. Katzin, Larry Peerce, Vincent McEveety, Bernard McEveety, Harry Harris, Marc Daniels; Music: Dominic Frontiere; Theme: Dominic Frontiere, Alan Alch.

CAST:

Jason McCord . . . . Chuck Connors
Ann Williams . . . . Lola Albright
Gen. Joshua McCord . . . . . John Carradine

Branded was the story of West Point graduate Jason McCord, a United States Army captain wrongfully branded a coward and scorned because he was the sole survivor of the Battle at Bitter Creek, Wyoming, in 1880. McCord defended himself by claiming he had been knocked unconscious during the attack. He was found guilty of desertion, stripped of his rank, and dishonorably discharged. Fortunately, during his trial, McCord was able to piece together a theory that he was framed by another officer who he was convinced deserted the Bitter Creek massacre. No one believed McCord's story so he began his own search in episode after episode, scouring the West in hope of clearing his name. McCord carried a six-shooter and the broken sword, which was the symbol of his dismissal from the Army.

Chuck Connors died November 10, 1992.
John Carradine died November 27, 1988.

Chuck Connors

THE LEGEND OF JESSE JAMES

Starring Christopher Jones and
Allen Case

CREDITS:

NBC: September 13, 1965 through September 5, 1966 (26 episodes); Produced by: 20th Century-Fox Television; Producer: Don Siegel; Music: Joseph Hooven.

CAST:

Jesse James . . . . Christopher Jones
Frank James . . . . Allen Case
Marshal Sam Corbett . . . . . Robert J. Wilke
Cole Younger . . . . John Milford

The Legend of Jesse James was, of course, not based on historical facts of the real outlaws of the Old West. It would have been nice, however, had they been the way this Western portrayed them. The show was filled with much color and excitement.

The setting for this Western was Saint Joseph, Missouri, in the 1860s during the times of Frank and Jesse James. These notorious outlaw brothers supposedly went into the life of crime and violence because railroad officials killed their mother after she refused to sell them her land. To avenge her death, Frank and Jesse became desperadoes robbing trains to get back at the railroad executives. Frank and Jesse made attempts to return any stolen goods to innocent victims of the railroad.

Producer/director Don Siegel turned these infamous bad guys into Robin Hood-like heroes in this season-long following of their exploits.

Allen Case died August 25, 1986.

Christopher Jones (left)
and Allen Case

170

A MAN CALLED SHENANDOAH

Starring Robert Horton

CREDITS:

ABC: September 14, 1965 through September 5, 1966 (34 episodes); Produced by: MGM Television; Executive Producers: Fred Freiberger, E. Jack Neuman, Vincent M. Fennelly; Director: Jerry Hopper; Creator: E.

Robert Horton

Jack Neuman; Music: George Stroll, Robert Van Eps; Theme Song Performer: Robert Horton.

CAST:

Shenandoah . . . . Robert Horton

A Man Called Shenandoah was both a unique Western and a suspense story of one nameless man seeking his own identity in 1877, an amnesiac who lost his memory from a gunshot wound to the head during an ambush. Being shot for unknown reasons and left to die on the desert, he is discovered by two bounty hunters. Thinking there might be a price on his head, they take him to the nearest town where a saloon girl named Kate (Beverly Garland, in the first episode) assists in his recovery. Unfortunately, after regaining consciousness, he is unaware of who he is or of any information about his own past which might lead to the discovery of his true identity.

He called himself Shenandoah, and his search began while wandering through the West. Shenandoah was a quiet man of action, but when troublemakers mistook his gentle disposition for timidity, they were usually in for a rude or perhaps fatal surprise.

LAREDO

Starring Neville Brand, Peter Brown, and William Smith

CREDITS:

NBC: September 16, 1965 through September 8, 1967 (56 episodes); Produced by: Universal Television; Executive producers: Howard Christie, Richard Irving; Producer: Frederick Sharr; Directors: Harvey Hart, Gene L. Coon, Bernard McEveety; Music: Stanley Wilson, Russell Garcia; Theme: Russ Garcia.

CAST:

Reese Bennett . . . . Neville Brand
Chad Cooper . . . . Peter Brown
Joe Riley . . . . William Smith
Capt. Ed Parmalee . . . . . . Philip Carey
Erik Hunter . . . . Robert Wolders

Laredo began as a spin-off from an episode of another popular Western, *The Virginian*. It was about the exploits of three rambunctious Texas Rangers and their captain, stationed in Laredo, Texas, in the 1870s.

The Texas Rangers of Company B—Reese Bennett, Chad Cooper, and Joe Riley—bickered and argued constantly over their misadventures while tracking down criminals wanted by the State of Texas. It was the comic overtones of these arguments, especially of grousing Reese Bennett, the veteran ranger, who seemed more intent at winning a point than dodging a bullet, which made this Western fun to watch.

Captain Parmalee, the rangers' superior, had his hands full looking after these jokesters, who always seemed to come through when the chips were down. It was always easy to see where they had been because of the destruction they left behind in their wake.

Neville Brand died April 16, 1992.

Neville Brand, William Smith, Peter Brown, and (seated) Philip Carey

THE IRON HORSE

Starring Dale Robertson

CREDITS:

ABC: September 12, 1966 through January 6, 1968 (47 episodes); Produced by: Dragonet Productions; Executive Producer: Matthew Rapf; Music: Dominic Frontiere.

CAST:

Ben Calhoun . . . . Dale Robertson
Dave Tarrant . . . . Gary Collins
Barnabas Rogers . . . . Bob Random

The setting was Wyoming during the 1870s for this exciting Western titled *The Iron Horse*. It was the story of Ben Calhoun, a rugged gentleman gambler, who won a railroad in a poker game; well, most of a railroad. Calhoun soon learned his newly acquired company, the Buffalo Pass, Scalplock, and Defiance Railroad, was only half built and almost in bankruptcy. The investors were impatient about the return of their money, which had been promised. It was now Ben Calhoun's responsibility to pay back the loans and restore the money to his creditors.

Ben contacted engineer Dave Tarrant; Nils, the giant crewman; Barnabas, his clerk; and a few other friends to help him finish building the railroad. Nothing was going to stop progress! Calhoun was dedicated and determined to make his Iron Horse a great success, but there were many problems along the route. Train

Dale Robertson

Dale Robertson in *The Iron Horse*

robbers, attacking Indians, and con men wanting in on Calhoun's fortune were all part of the problems that Ben Calhoun didn't bargain for.

SHANE

Starring David Carradine

CREDITS:

ABC: September 10, 1966 through December 31, 1966 (17 episodes); Produced by: ABC Television; Executive Producer: David Shaw; Producer: Herbert Brodkin; Directors: Robert Butler, David Shaw, Gary Nelson, Jud Taylor, Herschel Daugherty, Marc Daniels, Gerd Oswald; Music: Jerry Fielding; Theme: Victor Young.

CAST:

Shane	David Carradine
Marian Starrett	Jill Ireland
Joey Starrett	Christopher Shea
Tom Starrett	Tom Tully
Rufe Ryker	Bert Freed

Shane was a short-lived series (some four months) which was based on the book by Jack Schaefer and the classic 1953 film.

It told the story of a mysterious drifter who rode into a feud in the Wyoming Territory between the homesteading Starrett Family and the cattlemen who wanted their land. Shane objected to the pressure, which he had seen happen before, and opted to remain with the Starretts as a hired hand in their fight against Rufe Ryker, a particularly evil cattle baron.

Widowed Marian Starrett liked Shane and appreciated what he did for her, but she realized he would move on as he had before. Her son Joey idolized Shane and from the taciturn ex-gunslinger learned that a gun was not necessarily a weapon but a tool like a "plow or an ax" and only as good as the man behind it.

David Carradine

THE ROUNDERS

Starring Chill Wills

CREDITS:

ABC: September 6, 1966 through January 3, 1967 (17 episodes); Produced by: MGM Television; Executive Producer: Burt Kennedy; Producer: Ed Adamson; Director: Tom Gries; Music: Jeff Alexander.

David Carradine, John Qualen, and Sam Gilman in a scene from episode, "The Ha'nt"

None knew where Shane (played in the same silent, brooding mold by David Carradine as in his later *Kung Fu* series) came from or of his background, but they could feel his energy and power. And as one wise old-timer remarked, "He was like one of them there slow burning fires; took 'em a while, but you better watch out!"

Jill Ireland died May 18, 1990, and was the wife of actor Charles Bronson.

Chill Wills

176

CAST:

Ben Jones	Ron Hayes
Howdy Lewis	Patrick Wayne
Jim Ed Love	Chill Wills
Sally	Janis Hansen
Ada	Bobbi Jordan

The Rounders was a lighthearted contemporary Western based on Max Evans's novel and the Glenn Ford–Henry Fonda feature film (1965). This short-lived series starred Ron Hayes and Patrick Wayne, John's son. But perhaps the real star in this show was a Palomino horse named Old Fooler, who was more clever than wheeling-dealing Jim Ed Love, played by Chill Wills (who repeated his film role). Guest stars like Andy Devine and Strother Martin were the type of characters who appeared on *The Rounders* to fit the show's humor.

The show depicted the misadventures of two fun-loving cowpokes, Ben Jones and Howdy Lewis, employed as hands for crafty, white-suited Jim Ed Love,

the owner of the J.L. cattle ranch in Texas. Jim Ed didn't like to do business in a normal straightforward manner, but preferred to let himself be guided by his scheming instincts. Time and time again he is foiled in his connivings by the utter lack of gray matter in his two hired hands. Jim Ed could often be seen pulling his hair and grinding his teeth in frustration, saying to himself, "Them boys couldn't be that stupid."

Chill Wills died December 15, 1978.

THE MONROES

Starring Michael Anderson, Jr., and Barbara Hershey

CREDITS:

ABC: September 7, 1966 through August 30, 1967 (26 episodes); Produced by: ABC; Executive Producer: Frederick Brogger; Producer: Al C. Ward; Directors:

(From left) Kevin Schultz, Michael Anderson Jr., Barbara Hershey, Keith Schultz, and Tammy Locke (seated front)

Bernard Kowalski, Earl Bellamy, Robert Douglas, Tom Gries, Norman Foster, R.G. Springsteen; Music: Harry Sukman, Robert Drasnin; Theme: David Rose.

CAST:

Clayt Monroe	Michael Anderson, Jr.
Kathleen Monroe	Barbara Hershey
Amy Monroe	Tammy Locke
Fennimore Monroe	Kevin Schultz
Jefferson Monroe	Keith Schultz
Sleeve	Ben Johnson
Dirty Jim	Ron Soble
Major Mapoy	Liam Sullivan

This western concerned a family of pioneers, The Monroes: Albert, his wife Mary, and their five children: Clayt (age eighteen), Kathleen (age sixteen), the twin boys Jefferson and Fennimore (age twelve), and Amy (age six). Albert took his family to Wyoming in 1875 in search of land he had laid claim to ten years before. When they attempted to cross the dangerous Snake River, Albert and Mary drowned in the raging water, leaving the children as orphans. Teenage Clayt and Kathleen had to take responsibility for their younger sister and twin brothers, while fighting to establish a homestead in the rugged Wyoming Territory. (The series was filmed on location in Grand Teton National Park.)

Helping the Monroes attempt to fulfill their parents' dream by establishing their new homestead in the American West was Dirty Jim, a renegade Indian. Opposing them was nasty British cattle baron Major Mapoy, who wanted their land.

THE HIGH CHAPARRAL

Starring Leif Erickson

CREDITS:

NBC: September 10, 1967 through September 10, 1971 (96 episodes); Produced by: NBC; Executive Producer: David Dortort; Producers: William F. Claxton, James Schermer; Creator: David Dortort; Directors: Harry Harris, Corey Allen, Leon Benson, Herschel Daugherty, William F. Claxton, Joseph Pevney, William Wiard, William Witney; Music: Harry Sukman, David Rose.

Leif Erickson

CAST:

John Cannon	Leif Erickson
Buck Cannon	Cameron Mitchell
Victoria De Montoya Cannon . . .	Linda Cristal
Billy Blue Cannon	Mark Slade
Don Sebastian De Montoya . . .	Frank Silvera
Manolito De Montoya	Henry Darrow

NBC's most successful Western during the 1960s was arguably *The High Chaparral*, a series created by David Dortort, the man also responsible for *Bonanza*.

(Clockwise from left) Cameron Mitchell, Henry Darrow, Mark Slade, Leif Erickson, and Linda Cristal

This series was about the struggles of the Cannon family to maintain and protect their ranch, the High Chaparral, in lawless Tucson during the 1870s. There also was the neighboring spread of the landed Montoyas, a clan with Mexican roots in the Arizona Territory. The Cannon ranch was located in the middle of Apache Territory, to which the Indian leader Cochise did not take too kindly. As if trouble with Indians was not bad enough, there were always Mexican desperadoes to deal with. Big John led the Cannons through many lawless times, attempting to establish a successful cattle empire.

The High Chaparral was filmed on location in and around Old Tucson, Arizona, where the ranch setting stands today, twelve miles west of Tucson.

Leif Erickson died January 29, 1986.

The High Chaparral ranch set stands today in Old Tucson, famous Arizona movie location.

Linda Cristal and Leif Erickson

180

HONDO

Starring Ralph Taeger

CREDITS:

ABC: September 8, 1967 through December 29, 1967 (17 episodes); Produced by: Batjac Productions; Executive Producer: Andrew J. Fenady; Music: Richard Markowitz.

CAST:

Hondo Lane	. . . .	Ralph Taeger
Buffalo Baker	. . . .	Noah Beery, Jr.
Angie Dow	. . . .	Kathie Brown
Johnny Dow	. . . .	Buddy Foster
Chief Vittoro	. . . .	Michael Pate
Captain Richards	. . . .	Gary Clarke

Hondo was a relatively brief television series based on Louis L'Amour's bestseller and the character portrayed by John Wayne in the 1953 movie of the same name. *Hondo*, produced by John Wayne's company, Batjac, ran only a few months before being canceled.

The setting was Arizona Territory in the late 1860s, a violent time between the Indians and the white man. Troubleshooter Hondo Lane, a United States cavalry disptach rider headquartered at Fort Lowell, attempted to end the disputes and bloodshed between the two because of his trust for Apache Chief Vittoro. Once having lived with the Apaches, Hondo married Chief

Vittoro's daughter only to watch her die at the hands of the cavalry during a massacre. Hondo was a loner and went out on missions, encountering many assorted bad men, with his traveling companion Sam, his dog and best friend.

CIMARRON STRIP

Starring Stuart Whitman

CREDITS:

CBS: September 7, 1967 through September 19, 1968 (26 episodes); Produced by: CBS Television; Executive Producer: Philip Leacock; Producer: Bernard McEveety; Directors: Sam Wanamaker, Don Medford, Boris Sagal, Vincent McEveety, Lamont Johnson, Robert Butler; Music: Maurice Jarre, Morton Stevens.

CAST:

Marshal Jim Crown	Stuart Whitman
Dulcey Coopersmith	Jill Townsend
MacGregor	Percy Herbert
Francis Wilde	Randy Boone

Cimarron Strip was one of the top television Westerns produced in the late 1960s, as the cowboys began riding off into the sunset. This ninety-minute Western had all the ingredients for success, yet it still never received the credit it deserved. *Cimarron Strip* had a top-notch cast, beautiful scenery, action story lines, and an excellent lineup of guest stars like Richard Boone, Telly Savalas, Robert Duvall, Andrew Duggan,

Stuart Whitman

182

Photo: Courtesy of TV Guide

Stuart Whitman as U.S. Marshal Jim Crown

THE GUNS OF WILL SONNETT

Starring Walter Brennan and Dack Rambo

CREDITS:

ABC: September 8, 1967 through September 15, 1969 (50 episodes); Produced by: Thomas–Spelling Productions; Executive Producer: Danny Thomas; Producer: Aaron Spelling; Directors: Thomas Carr, Jean Yarbrough, Michael O'Herlihy; Music: Fred Steiner, Earle Hagen; Theme: Earle Hagen, Hugo Friedhofer.

Walter Brennan and Dack Rambo

Warren Oates, and others. CBS even hired top directors from *Gunsmoke* and began to rebroadcast the series in 1971, but it fizzled out in September of that year.

The series dramatized the exploits of rugged U.S. Marshal Jim Crown, patroling the ten-million-acre stretch of land between Oklahoma and Kansas, known as the Cimarron Strip, and attempting to settle range wars between the settlers and the cattlemen along the route. Marshal Crown crossed paths with many outlaws and bad guys during this violent era of the 1880s. In addition to his patrol, he had to keep an eye on Cimarron City and the cowboys passing through. Crown only had two part-time deputies, a Scotsman named MacGregor, and a young photographer, Francis Wilde, to aid him in keeping law and order in Cimarron. Perky Dulcey Coopersmith, who ran the Wayfarer's Inn Hotel where the marshal lived, was in love with him, but he thought of her more as his younger sister. Such was often the plight of beautiful women in television Westerns.

183

CAST:

Will Sonnett	Walter Brennan
Jeff Sonnett	Dack Rambo
James Sonnett	Jason Evers

The Guns of Will Sonnett told the weekly adventures of a grizzled ex-cavalry scout and his grandson Jeff, abandoned as an infant by his father during the 1860s. The setting was Wyoming in the 1870s where a search began to find Jeff's father, James Sonnett, a wanted gunman who had deserted his family. Jeff, who is twenty and grown to manhood, learned of his father's reputation as a gunslinger through people who knew him and the dusty trail he left behind.

Jeff's strong determination to find his father increased on discovering that he and his grandfather were not the only ones tracking the gunfighter and that time was running out. Jeff and Will encountered an endless array of trouble with bounty hunters and other gunmen who had unfinished business to settle with Sonnett. The two were both fast with a six-gun; anytime someone questioned that, Will would state, "No brag, just fact." Sometimes those were the last four words the opposing gunslinger ever heard.

The Guns of Will Sonnett had a successful run on ABC, although the Sonnetts hadn't met up with their kin when the show was canceled. In the final episode, Will and Jeff came upon a man who claimed that he had killed James Sonnett in a gunfight.

Walter Brennan died September 21, 1974.

Walter Brennan in *The Guns of Will Sonnett*

CUSTER

Starring Wayne Maunder

CREDITS:

ABC: September 6, 1967 through December 27, 1967 (17 episodes); Produced by: 20th Century-Fox Television; Executive Producer: David Weisbart; Producer: Frank Glicksman; Director: Norman Foster; Music: Richard Markowitz, Elmer Bernstein, Leith Stevens, Joseph Mullendore.

CAST:

Col. George Armstrong Custer .	Wayne Maunder
Joe Miller, trail scout	Slim Pickens
Capt. Myles Keogh	Grant Woods
Sgt. James Bustard	Peter Palmer
Gen. Alfred Terry	Robert F. Simon
Chief Crazy Horse	Michael Dante

Custer stands as one of television's most controversial Westerns, perhaps because it tried to glorify Custer's ruthless killing of the Cheyennes. Mercifully, the show was short-lived on ABC.

This series (alternately known as *The Legend of Custer*) was set in Kansas in 1867 where Maj. Gen. George Armstrong Custer of the U.S. cavalry was found guilty of dereliction of duty and reduced in rank to Lieutenant Colonel. Custer was sent to Fort Hays, where he was put in charge of a labor battalion humorously known as "The Fighting Seventh." Custer had a personal war going with Crazy Horse, a Sioux Indian chief, as well as with the Cheyenne tribe. Custer refused to treat his unit as a work detail and trained them to become the sorriest cavalrymen the West has

(Standing from left) Peter Palmer, Robert F. Simon, Wayne Maunder, Grant Woods;
(front) Slim Pickens and Michael Dante.

185

Wayne Maunder

Producer: Hugh Benson; Producer: Jon Epstein; Director: E. W. Swackhamer; Music: Hugo Montenegro.

CAST:

Earl Corey	Don Murray
Jemal David	Otis Young

By 1968, television had become more open to violence and realism than ever before, as in this short-lived "salt

ever seen. Leathery Indian scout Joe Miller was Custer's sidekick of sorts, General Terry the fort's commanding officer, and Captain Keogh the witty Irishman with whom Custer could share drinks.

Slim Pickens died November 8, 1983.

THE OUTCASTS

Starring Don Murray and Otis Young

CREDITS:

ABC: September 23, 1968 through September 15, 1969 (26 episodes); Produced by: Screen Gems; Executive

and pepper" television Western. Few will remember this single-season series that aired on ABC, but none should forget the blood and guts it portrayed.

It was the story of two outcasts of the post-Civil War era. Earl Corey, a white Virginia aristocrat turned gambler and drifter, and Jemal David, a former slave, teamed up reluctantly as professional bounty hunters. Needless to say, neither trusted the other; in fact, they actually hated one another. Quite often arguments led to fistfights, and God help any man trying to settle one of their private disputes. They may have had an inborn dislike of each other, fastened by the decaying aristocracy of the Southern social structure, but there still remained an honest appreciation and respect of one man for the other in this violent but unique television Western about two antagonistic cowboys—one white, one black—tracking down criminals for the money.

Otis Young in *The Outcasts*

Otis Young and Don Murray

187

LANCER

Starring Andrew Duggan

CREDITS:

CBS: September 24, 1968 through September 8, 1970 (51 episodes); Produced by: 20th Century-Fox Television; Producers: Sam Wanamaker, Alan A. Armer; Directors: Don McDougall, Leo Penn, Alexander Singer, Gene Nelson, Sam Wanamaker, Christian I. Nyby, Robert Butler, William Hale; Music: Joseph Mullendore, Hugo Friedhofer; Theme: Jerome Moross.

CAST:

Murdoch Lancer	Andrew Duggan
Scott Lancer	Wayne Maunder
Johnny Madrid Lancer	James Stacy
Teresa O'Brian	Elizabeth Baur
Jelly Hoskins	Paul Brinegar

Lancer was another lively Western about a ranch, in *The High Chaparral–Bonanza* mold. However, it had its own different story line, telling of the efforts of Murdoch Lancer, a widower, and Teresa, his young ward, to protect their 100,000-acre cattle and timberland property located in the San Joaquin Valley of California during the 1870s.

The older Murdoch struggled against land pirates who knew he could no longer fight the bad guys alone. It seemed every time he hired extra help, they were either killed or told to get out while they still could. Murdoch found himself turning to his two sons, Johnny Madrid, a drifting gunslinger, and Scott, a college student in Boston. Both sons were by different

Andrew Duggan

188

James Stacy, Andrew Duggan, Wayne Maunder, Elizabeth Baur, and Paul Brinegar (seated)

marriages and had never met. The Lancers, along with ranch foreman Jelly Hoskins, a cranky old-timer, continued their fight successfully through three seasons of *Lancer*, the final one of which was made up entirely of reruns.

Andrew Duggan died May 15, 1988.

ALIAS SMITH & JONES

Starring Peter Deuel and Ben Murphy

CREDITS:

ABC: January 21, 1971 through January 13, 1973 (48 episodes); Produced by: Universal Television; Execu-

Ben Murphy and Peter Deuel in *Alias Smith & Jones*

Peter Deuel (left) and Ben Murphy

Ben Murphy and Peter Deuel in *Alias Smith & Jones*

tive Producer: Roy Huggins; Creator/Producer: Glen A. Larson; Directors: Bruce Kessler, Barry Shear, Arnold Laven, Douglas Heyes, Jeffrey Hayden, Jack Arnold, Gene Leavitt; Music: Billy Goldenberg, Robert Prince.

CAST:

Hannibal Hayes alias Joshua
   Smith . . . . Peter Deuel (later Roger Davis)
Jed "Kid" Curry alias
   Thaddeus Jones . . . . Ben Murphy
Clementine Hale . . . . Sally Field

Alias Smith & Jones was one of the best Westerns to hit television in the 1970s. This lighthearted series followed in the footsteps of *Butch Cassidy and the Sundance Kid*, which starred Robert Redford and Paul Newman.

Hannibal Hayes, alias Joshua Smith, and Jed "Kid" Curry, alias Thaddeus Jones, were two amiable ex-bank robbers trying to give up the life of crime and go straight to clear their names. They had been promised full pardons by the governor if they could stay out of trouble for at least one year. That could be hard to do, since every lawman, bounty hunter, and outlaw had a score to settle with these two characters. Smith and

191

Ben Murphy and Peter Deuel in a familiar scene from *Alias Smith & Jones*

Ben Murphy and Peter Deuel

192

Peter Deuel in a scene from *Alias Smith & Jones*

Jones roamed through Kansas Territory, often with another lovable rogue, Clementine Hale (for feminine interest)—played by Sally Field in her post-*Flying Nun/Gidget* days—valiantly trying to keep clear of their former outlaw gangs to protect their pardons and to stay away from illegal business opportunities. It wasn't easy.

Peter Deuel committed suicide December 31, 1971, at age thirty-one.

Roger Davis, the show's unseen narrator to the time, replaced Peter Deuel in the final episodes of the series.

193

HEC RAMSEY

Starring Richard Boone

CREDITS:

NBC: October 8, 1972 through August 25, 1974 (10 episodes); Produced by: Mark VII Ltd. Productions; Executive Producer: Jack Webb; Producers: Douglas Benton, Harold Jack Bloom; Directors: Harry Morgan, Richard Quine, Andrew V. McLaglen, George Marshall, Nicholas Colasanto; Music: Fred Steiner, Lee Holdridge; Theme: Henry Mancini; Narrator: Harry Morgan.

CAST:

Deputy Hec Ramsey	Richard Boone
Sheriff Oliver B. Stamp	Richard Lenz
Doc Amos Coogan	Harry Morgan
Norma Muldoon	Sharon Acker

Hec Ramsey was one of NBC's alternating *Sunday Mystery Movie* segments in the early 1970s. A grizzled ex-gunfighter, Ramsey ended up in New Prospect, Oklahoma, in the early 1900s working as a deputy sheriff. When he arrived in town, he discovered the

Richard Boone

Richard Boone as Hec Ramsey

sheriff, Oliver B. Stamp, to be a young and inexperienced whippersnapper. Sheriff Stamp had heard about Hec Ramsey's legendarily fast gun, and was certain his reputation for causing trouble would follow him to his newly appointed post. Though Sheriff Stamp was uneasy at first, he and Ramsey eventually worked very well together.

Hec Ramsey was a unique lawman with an unusual flair for solving crimes with what he called the "Newfangled Science of Criminology." Having been studying new methods of law enforcement, Ramsey became increasingly dependent on a trunkful of detective paraphernalia, including magnifying glasses, scales, dusting powder, fingerprinting equipment, and other gadgets of modern-day criminology needed to track down his suspects. Ramsey still continued wearing his six-gun, but his new techniques of investigating crimes provided the show's lighthearted Western mystery.

Richard Boone died January 10, 1981.

Richard Boone, Susan Keener, and Harry Morgan in a scene from *Hec Ramsey*

KUNG FU

Starring David Carradine

CREDITS:

ABC: October 14, 1972 through June 27, 1975 (72 episodes); Produced by: Warner Brothers Television; Executive Producer: Jerry Thorpe; Producers: John Furia, Jr., Alex Beaton, Herman Miller; Creator: Ed Spielman; Directors: Barry Crane, Charles Dubin, Robert Totten, David Carradine, Robert Michael Lewis, Walter Doniger, Robert Butler, Richard Lang, Gordon Hessler, Harry Harris, John Llewellyn Moxey; Music: Jim Helms.

CAST:

Kwai Chang Caine	David Carradine
Danny Caine, Kwai's half-brother .	Tim McIntire
Margit McLean, Caine's cousin .	Season Hubley
Master Po	Keye Luke
Master Kan	Philip Ahn
Master Teh	John Leoning
Caine, as a boy	Radames Pera

David Carradine in
Kung Fu

196

David Carradine and Keye Luke

Kung Fu was an unusual Western and had a very successful run on ABC. The 1970s saw the rage of martial arts in movies with Bruce Lee and others, therefore, creating a new background for *Kung Fu*. Do not be misled in thinking the character in *Kung Fu* was a Chinese gunfighter, although this seemed to be what

television viewers expected before the show made its debut.

Kung Fu revealed the exploits of Kwai Chang Caine, a Chinese American Buddhist, training to become a Shaolin priest. In search of a lost brother, Caine set out on a journey across the American Frontier during the 1870s. He was forced to kill a royal nephew during a fight which took the life of his favorite martial-arts teacher, Master Po, who stayed with Caine in spirit through the run of the show. Caine then had a price on his head, and a large reward was posted throughout the West, making it difficult for him to elude the bounty hunters. Fortunately, his lessons in the art of kung fu prepared him for self-protection as well as enabled him to help others in distress along his travels. A man of few words, he could always expect trouble with gunslingers and disrespectful cowboys who learned too late their mistake challenging Caine to a showdown.

In the nineties, *Kung Fu* was successfully revived on Fox Television, with Carradine returning briefly to assist the grandson of Caine, who was also being pursued weekly.

LITTLE HOUSE ON THE PRAIRIE

Starring Michael Landon

CREDITS:

NBC: September 11, 1974 through September 21, 1982; Produced by: NBC Entertainment; Executive Produc-

Michael Landon

The cast of *Little House on the Prairie*

ers: Michael Landon, Ed Friendly; Producers: John Hawkins, William F. Claxton, B.W. Saudefur, Winston Miller, Kent McCray; Directors: Michael Landon, Maury Dexter, Victor French, Leo Penn, Alf Kjellin, B.W. Sandefur, William F. Claxton, Lewis Allen; Music: David Rose.

CAST:

Charles Ingalls	Michael Landon
Caroline Ingalls	Karen Grassle
Laura Ingalls	Melissa Gilbert
Mary Ingalls	Melissa Sue Anderson
Carrie Ingalls	Sidney Greenbush/
	Lindsay Greenbush
Isaiah Edwards	Victor French
Dr. Baker	Kevin Hagen

Michael Landon wrote, produced, often directed, and starred in the hugely popular but mild Western, *Little House on the Prairie*, based on the novels by Laura Ingalls Wilder of the same title. As young Laura Ingalls, Melissa Gilbert narrated the stories of Laura's formative years with her family on the prairie. *Little House* remains one of television's most respected programs because of its family-oriented themes and the values it depicted.

It told of the Charles Ingalls family and their triumphs in Plumb Creek, a small community located near Walnut Grove, Minnesota, during the 1870s. Charles, his wife Caroline, and their three young daughters were pioneers who struggled through many hard times trying to overcome various disasters. Some of the problems the Ingalls faced were crop failure due to severe weather conditions, deadly diseases, shortage of work, and an infestation of desperadoes. The Ingalls also had their share of ornery, low-down varmints who lived in the same community. On the other hand, the Ingalls were blessed with several good neighbors and friends who always were ready to lend a hand in emotional times. One such friend in the show, Isaiah Edwards, a neighbor, was portrayed by veteran actor Victor French, who became Michael Landon's best friend in real life.

When Michael Landon tired of doing the series, he created a spin-off called *Little House: A New Beginning,* focusing entirely on the Melissa Gilbert character. It ran during the 1982–83 season. There followed three final two-hour television movies that tied up loose strings and literally leveled the town of Walnut Creek.

Michael Landon died July 1, 1991.

Victor French died June 13, 1989.

THE BARBARY COAST

Starring William Shatner and Doug McClure

CREDITS:

ABC: September 8, 1975 through January 9, 1976 (13 episodes); Produced by: ABC; Executive Producer: Cy Chermak; Producer: Douglas Heyes; Directors: Bill Bixby, Don McDougall, Don Weis, Alex Grasshoff, Herb Wallerstein; Music: John Andrew Tartaglia, George Aliceson Tipton.

CAST:

Jeff Cable	William Shatner
Cash Conover	Doug McClure
Moose Moran, bouncer	Richard Kiel
Thumbs, piano player	Dave Turner

William Shatner and Doug McClure teamed up together for this short-lived Western series, *The Barbary Coast.*

The Barbary Coast dealt with the adventures of Jeff Cable and Cash Conover, respectively, a rugged undercover federal agent who was a master of disguises and a flamboyant, appropriately named casino owner. (No wonder the series originally was to be titled *Cash & Cable.*) They worked hand in glove to apprehend crooks on San Francisco's wild and untamed Barbary Coast of the 1880s.

Cable lived in a secret luxury apartment hidden behind a wall of Conover's gambling casino. His investigations for the governor of California were only known by his partner Conover and the governor himself. Cable never left his cozy digs without a disguise when trying to unravel crime cases and undo evil, and invariably seemed to be able to persuade Conover to assist him on his undercover capers, despite the latter's constant protestation, "This is *positively* the last time." Then, in the next episode, we see Conover coerced once again by the ingenious Cable, reluctantly shaking his head with resignation as he follows his partner from one life-threatening situation to another, dealing with unscrupulous varmints, flashy ladies, and sourdoughs.

William Shatner

Doug McClure (left) and William Shatner in *Barbary Coast*

HOW THE WEST WAS WON

Starring James Arness

CREDITS:

ABC: February 12, 1977 through April 23, 1979 (26 episodes); Executive Producer: John Mantley; Producers: Jeffrey Hayden, John G. Stephens; Directors: Burt Kennedy, Daniel Mann, Vincent McEveety, Bernard McEveety, Alf Kjellin, Harry Falk; Music: Jerrold Immel, Bruce Broughton, John Parker; Narrator: William Conrad.

CAST:

Zeb Macahan	James Arness
Kate Macahan	Eva Marie Saint
Luke Macahan	Bruce Boxleitner
Laura Macahan	Kathryn Holcomb
Jessie Macahan	Vicki Schreck
Josh Macahan	William Kirby Cullen
Timothy Macahan	Richard Kiley
Molly Culhane	Fionnula Flanagan

James Arness, *Gunsmoke's* legendary Marshal Matt Dillon, returned to television for another successful Western in *How the West Was Won*. When the pilot for this series was shown as a 1976 television movie, it was called *The Macahans*. ABC changed the title to *How the West Was Won* when the series debuted. It ran in fits and starts: three episodes in 1977, twelve in 1978, eleven in 1979.

How the West Was Won concerned the struggles and hardships of mountain man Zeb Macahan, a trapper and hunter for nearly ten years in the Dakota Territory during the 1860s, and vaguely based on the character Henry Fonda played in the all-star 1962 Western film of the same title. Because of the American western expansion, however, the wilds were vanishing, and Zeb's way of life was changed. He decided to return to his homeland in Virginia to join his brother

James Arness

203

Timothy and his family, who were leaving in a covered wagon heading west to seek a better life. The Macahans had just begun their journey West when the Civil War broke out. Timothy and his wife Kate had to go back east. Upon their return, they were killed in an accident, leaving Zeb with the four children: Luke, Laura, Jessie, and Josh. Zeb found out later that Luke was on the run for killing three gunslingers. Although the shootings were in self-defense, Luke was wanted by lawmen and bounty hunters throughout the land. Kate's sister Molly, a widow from Boston, decided to join Zeb and help with the family's difficult times.

How the West Was Won was a Western in the grand old frontier style.

James Arness as Zeb Macahan in *How The West Was Won*

THE OREGON TRAIL

Starring Rod Taylor

The cast of *How The West Was Won*

CREDITS:

NBC: September 21, 1977 through October 26, 1977 (13 episodes; only 6 shown); Produced by: Universal Television; Executive Producer: Michael Gleason; Producer: Carl Vitale; Directors: Virgil W. Vogel, Bill Bixby, Don Richardson; Music: Dick DeBenedictis; Theme Song Performer: Danny Darst.

CAST:

Evan Thorpe	Rod Taylor
Andrew Thorpe	Andrew Stevens
Rachel Thorpe	Gina Maria Smika
William Thorpe	Tony Becker
Margaret Devlin	Darleen Carr
Luther Sprague	Charles Napier

The Oregon Trail was a very short-lived television Western continuation of the television movie of the same title. Thirteen episodes of this series were filmed but the show was put out to pasture after only six episodes were aired. During the 1970s when *The Oregon Trail* was shown, there appeared to be waning interest in Westerns, but the show's low ratings were no reflection on its popular leading star, rugged Rod Taylor. *The Oregon Trail* also featured an array of top-name guest stars, such as Stella Stevens, James Wainwright, and Claude Akins, and was directed by Bill Bixby and other top directors. So what happened?

The story told of a courageous pioneer, Evan Thorpe, who, disillusioned, pulled up stakes with his family of three children and headed West on a wagon train from his native Illinois to Oregon. The Thorpes hoped to find a better life, but on their trek they faced many hardships stemming from Indian attacks to dreadful diseases. Evan Thorpe not only fought outside difficulties but had conflicts from the inner circle with an unfriendly scout, Luther Sprague. Fortunately, one of his passengers was pretty Margaret Devlin, whose beauty and charm managed to soften the rough and rocky Oregon Trail.

Rod Taylor in *The Oregon Trail*

THE YOUNG MAVERICK

Starring Charles Frank

CREDITS:

CBS: December 28, 1979 through January 16, 1980 (13 episodes/only 8 aired); Produced by: Warner Brothers Television; Executive Producer: Robert Van Scoyk; Producer: Chuck Bowman; Directors: Bernard McEveety, Don McDougall, Leslie H. Martinson, Ralph Senensky, Hy Averback; Music: Lee Holdridge, Lex DeAvezedo; Theme: Jay Livingston, Ray Evans.

CAST:

Ben Maverick	Charles Frank
Marshal Edge Troy	John Dehner
Nell McGarrahan	Susan Blanchard

The short-lived *The Young Maverick* was intended to be a continuation of the original *Maverick* series that ran from 1957 to 1962. However, *The Young Maverick*

Susan Blanchard and Charles Frank in *The Young Maverick*

Charles Frank, James Garner, and Jack Kelly in the pilot *The Young Maverick*

was canceled in the first season after only a few episodes. The explanation: poor ratings.

The pilot for this effort reunited the original Mavericks, James Garner and Jack Kelly, for the first time since 1960 in their famous roles of Bret and Bart. The two appeared only in the pilot to introduce Ben, the youngest Maverick, to give the show a boost in its debut.

Ben was the son of Beauregard Maverick (Roger Moore in the original series), Bret and Bart's British cousin. The disarming Ben was educated at Harvard and was inexperienced as a gambler. He tried to carry on the Maverick tradition by seeking his fortune at a poker table, while regularly attempting to avoid getting gunned down on the rough frontier. With his romantic interest Nell McGarrahan, he was mostly interested in traveling con games. Ben's luck ran out on January 16, 1980, when the show was canceled.

BRET MAVERICK

Starring James Garner

CREDITS:

NBC: December 1, 1981 through August 8, 1982 (18 episodes); Produced by: Warner Brothers Television; Executive Producer: Meta Rosenberg; Producers: Chas. Floyd Johnson, Geoffrey Fischer; Directors: Ivan Dixon, Stuart Margolin, Rod Holcomb, Leo Penn, William F. Claxton, William Wiard; Music: Murray McLeod, J.A.C. Redford; Theme Song Performer: Ed Bruce.

CAST:

Bret Maverick	James Garner
Mary Lou Springer	Darleen Carr
Philo Sandine	Stuart Margolin
Tom Guthrie	Ed Bruce
Cy Whitaker	Richard Hamilton
Elijah Crow, the banker	Raymond Bieri
Jack, the bartender	Jack Garner

Bret Maverick was an attempt (the third) to pick up where the original *Maverick* series in the 1950s left off, but it failed in the ratings, despite the strong presence of James Garner. The studio and film lot were the same, as were the character and the star, so what went wrong? There were a couple things different: the network was now NBC instead of ABC, and Bret had tired of roaming from town to town looking for a poker game. Whatever the reasons, the show didn't survive, although it was a good series, and Maverick's a durable character. Why else would he be resurrected for the big screen in 1994?

Bret was now less adventuresome ("twenty years older and forty years wiser") and had settled down in Sweetwater, Arizona, after winning the Lazy Ace ranch, The Red Ox saloon, and $50,000 in a poker game. Tom Guthrie became Bret's partner in the Red Ox after losing his reelection as sheriff. Bret was constantly being taken by the wacky, scheming Philo Sandine, who was a self-styled Indian scout and small-time con man. Another pain in the side for Bret was the fiesty Mary Lou Springer, photographer for the local newspaper *The Territorian* who constantly dragged Bret into trouble.

James Garner

210

Ed Bruce and James Garner in *Bret Maverick*

THE YOUNG RIDERS

Starring Ty Miller, Stephen Baldwin, Josh Brolin, Travis Fine, Gregg Rainwater, and Yvonne Suhor

CREDITS:

ABC: September 20, 1989 through May 30, 1992; Produced by: Ogiens-Kane Productions, Paragon Entertainment, and MGM/United Artists Television; Executive Producer: Jonas McCord; Producer: Christopher Seitz; Directors: Virgil W. Vogel, George Mendeluk; Music: John Debney.

CAST:

The "Kid"	Ty Miller
Teaspoon Hunter	Anthony Zerbe
Billy Cody	Stephen Baldwin
Jimmy Hickok	Josh Brolin
Ike McSwain	Travis Fine
Little Buck	Gregg Rainwater
Lou McCloud	Yvonne Suhor
Marshal Cain	Brett Cullen
Emma Shannon (first season) . . .	Melissa Leo
Noah Dixon (second season) . . .	Don Franklin
Rachel Dunne (second season) . .	Clare Wren

Gregg Rainwater, Stephen Baldwin, Ty Miller, Josh Brolin, Travis Fine, and Yvonne Suhor

On the spurred heels of the motion picture, *The Young Guns*, came a television Western in 1989, *The Young Riders*. This series, along with *Paradise* (still in production); successful television Western miniseries, such as *Lonesome Dove;* and the *Desperado*, *Gunsmoke*, and Kenny Rogers's "Gambler" television movies were greatly responsible for reviving the Western interest after a fallow spell. *The Young Riders* was seen on ABC Wednesday nights when the show began and appealed mainly to a young audience. It held its own in the ratings until the second season in 1990, when it was moved to Saturday nights, better known as the "death pit." Somehow, *The Young Riders* kept riding even into a third season but later rode off during the fall schedule in 1992.

The Young Riders was the story about five young lads and a female, disguised as a boy, recruited by a grizzly old codger named Teaspoon Hunter to be riders for the pony express. These young buckaroos, looking barely old enough to wear a gun, were put on a mail schedule by Teaspoon, and away they went. The run was from St. Joseph, Missouri, to Sacramento, California—2,000 miles, making for a long hard ride and a lot of hard work. The young riders hired by Teaspoon included Jimmy Hickok, who later in history became known as "Wild" Bill Hickok; Billy Cody, who became the famous Buffalo Bill Cody; Little Buck, a half-breed Indian; Ike, the bald-headed mute; one fast-with-a-gun rider known as the "Kid"; and Lou, the female disguised as a young boy to protect her job as a pony express rider. The riders traveled seventy-five miles a day, passing through 190 relay stations, delivering the mail despite assorted ambushes, Indian attacks, and bad guys with devious plans.

PARADISE

Starring Lee Horsley

CREDITS:

CBS: October 27, 1988 through June 14, 1991; Produced by: Lorimar Productions, Roundelay Productions; Executive Producer: David Jacobs; Producer: James H. Brown; Creators: David Jacobs, Robert Porter; Directors: David Jacobs, Joe Scanlan, Robert Scheerer, Michael Caffey, Kim Manners; Music: Jerrold Immel.

CAST:

Ethan Allen Cord	Lee Horsley
Amelia Lawson	Sigrid Thornton
Claire Carroll	Jenny Beck
Joseph Carroll	Matthew Newmark
Ben Carroll	Brian Lando
George Carroll	Michael Patrick Carter
John Taylor	Dehl Berti
Marshal P.J. Breckenhaous	Nicolas Surovy

Lee Horsley as Ethan Allen Cord

Paradise was a television Western originally written as a miniseries on CBS but instead developed into a weekly series.

It followed stalwart Ethan Allen Cord, a gunfighter exploiting his talent during the 1890s in the small mining town of Paradise, California. Cord was a loner until his sister suddenly died, leaving four motherless children: Joseph, Ben, George, and Claire to his responsibility. With a reputation as a gunslinger, Cord found it very difficult taking on a family. He was disliked by not only the people of Paradise but those of other towns as well.

Cord was forced to try settling down on a ranch outside of Paradise to make the best of raising the kids

Lee Horsley

the only way he knew how. He hired on as a guard at a worthless old mine. Meanwhile, with his lightning draw of a six-gun, Cord was fighting other battles on the other side of Paradise. The crooked town marshal, P.J. Breckenhaous, finally had to leave town, after being exposed to the citizenry, rather than face Cord's Colt .45.

John Taylor, one of Cord's few friends, was always around for backup when trouble appeared. Cord, however, did meet another true friend in Paradise, the beautiful Amelia Lawson, proprietor of the local bank, and they became attracted to each other. We didn't expect Cord to keep spending all his time with John Taylor did we?

The show was renamed *The Guns of Paradise* during its last season in an unsuccess attempt to boost the ratings. Memorable episodes of *Paradise* featured familiar guest stars from classic television Westerns of the 1950s, such as Chuck Connors of *The Rifleman*, Robert Fuller of *Wagon Train*, and Gene Barry and Hugh O'Brian reprising their roles of Bat Masterson and Wyatt Earp.

DR. QUINN, MEDICINE WOMAN

Starring Jane Seymour

CREDITS:

CBS: January 16, 1993–   ; Produced by: The Sullivan Company; Executive Producer: Beth Sullivan; Producers: Robert Gros, Arthur Seidé, Timothy Johnson;

Joe Lando, Jane Seymour, Shawn Toovey, Erika Flores, and Chad Allen in *Dr. Quinn, Medicine Woman*

Jane Seymour as Dr. Michaela Quinn

Brian . . . . Shawn Toovey
Colleen . . . . Erika Flores
Horace . . . . Frank Collison
Loren Bray . . . . Orson Bean

Dr. Quinn, Medicine Woman provided an *actress* with a starring role in a television Western for the first time since Barbara Stanwyck in *The Big Valley* and Brenda Vaccaro in *Sara*.

With British actress Jane Seymour, heretofore television's queen of prime-time romantic dramas, in the title role, *Dr. Quinn, Medicine Woman* is the story of Michaela Quinn, a woman doctor from back east who

Joe Lando and Jane Seymour

Directors: Chuck Bowman, Brenda Kalosh, John Liberti, James Keach, Rob Mendel; Music: William Olvis.

CAST:

Dr. Michaela Quinn . . . . . . Jane Seymour
Sully . . . . Joe Lando
Matthew . . . . Chad Allen

217

is tired of the way the medical establishment is being run and decides to look for job opportunities on the frontier. She finds herself in Colorado Springs in the 1880s, and no sooner does she arrive than she finds herself adopting an orphan family of three: Brian, Colleen, and Matthew. The people of Colorado Springs had sent for a doctor, and they assumed that Dr. Mike Quinn was a man. On her arrival, she discovers that the townsfolk don't cotton to lady doctors and realizes she has more than the medical challenges to overcome.

Dr. Michaela Quinn, a living testimony to sexual equality, speaks firmly against racial discrimination and strongly supports gun control—proving herself somewhat of a feminist a hundred years ahead of her time.

A half-breed tracker named Sully proves to be her one ally initially in the series, which became surprisingly popular, especially with the women audiences.

Just think, if the 1880s had been as pure as Dr. Michaela, there might not have been a wild, wild West. Then, on the other hand, there would not be a *Dr. Quinn, Medicine Woman* on Saturday nights.

THE ADVENTURES OF BRISCO COUNTY, JR.

Starring Bruce Campbell

Bruce Campbell in *Brisco County, Jr.*

CREDITS:

FOX-TV: August 27, 1993– ; Produced by: Boam/ Cuse Productions, Warner Brothers Television; Executive Producers: Jeffrey Boam, Carlton Cuse; Producers: Paul Marks, David Simkins, Brad Kern, John Wirth, Tom Chehak; Directors: Daniel Attias, James Contner, Johanna Jensen, Michael J. Pendell, Bryan Spicer; Music: Stephen Graziano, Randy Edelman.

CAST:

Brisco County, Jr.	Bruce Campbell
Lord Bowler	Julius Carry
Socrates Poole	Christian Clemenson
Dixie	Kelly Rutherford
John Bly	Billy Drago
Professor Wickwire	John Astin
Marshal Brisco, Sr.	R. Lee Ermey

Following a number of dry seasons, this became the biggest hit Western series to take the reins on television in the 1990s, in the style somewhere between *Maverick* and the comic movie adventures of Indiana Jones. The guns and the ratings are smoking in this wild and woolly Western. *Brisco* needs a wagonload of supplies and ammunition to survive. You have to think sometimes when watching that the characters of Brisco and Indiana Jones are very similar. Maybe the reason for this is that Jeffery Boam is the writer of both.

The Adventures of Brisco County, Jr. is a series about a Harvard-educated attorney who is hired as a bounty hunter by five robber barons to bring down the Bly gang, the scurvy villains who gunned down Brisco's lawman father. Each weekly episode carries an element of wild West adventure, including doses of suspense, humor, romance, and triumphs. Sticking close to Brisco, trying to protect his job and the company's investment, can be found Socrates Poole, the bookkeeper for the barons. However, with Socrates's lack of knowledge of the West, Brisco is usually the one found doing the protecting. Also riding as reluctant sidekick is Lord Bowler, a black rival bounty hunter who hooked up with Brisco for the hunt. Unlike Brisco, a hunter with a heart, Bowler joined forces for business—the reward. Together they manage to bring emotions and action to the screen. The bowler-hatted Bowler is somehow always looking out from behind the bars of a jail cell, down the barrel of a .44, or into the eyes of a rattlesnake. Often seen shooting to the rescue is Brisco's fun-loving horse Comet. Along the trail Brisco finds his way into the hearts of assorted romantic interests, a high-school sweetheart and other old flames as well as new sparks of fire. But there are always the assorted grungy varmints that help give the show its spark.

Bruce Campbell in *Brisco County, Jr.*

219

INDEX

(Italicized numbers indicate photos)

ORDER NOW!
Citadel Film, Television and Music Books

If you like this book, you'll love the other titles in the award-winning Citadel Film Series, as well as our television and movie books.

From James Stewart to Moe Howard and The Three Stooges, Woody Allen to John Wayne, The Citadel Film Series is America's largest and oldest film book library. With more than 150 titles--and more on the way!--Citadel Film Books make perfect gifts for a loved one, a friend, or best of all, yourself!

A complete listing of the Citadel Film Series appears below.
If you know what books you want, why not order now!
It's easy! Just call 1-800-447-BOOK and have your MasterCard or Visa ready.

STARS

Alan Ladd
Arnold Schwarzenegger
Barbra Streisand: First Decade
Barbra Streisand: Second Decade
The Barbra Streisand Scrapbook
Bela Lugosi
Bette Davis
The Bowery Boys
Brigitte Bardot
Buster Keaton
Carole Lombard
Cary Grant
Charlie Chaplin
Clark Gable
Clint Eastwood
Curly
Dustin Hoffman
Edward G. Robinson
Elizabeth Taylor
Elvis Presley
The Elvis Scrapbook
Errol Flynn
Frank Sinatra
Gary Cooper
Gene Kelly
Gina Lollobrigida
Gloria Swanson
Gregory Peck
Greta Garbo
Henry Fonda
Humphrey Bogart
Ingrid Bergman
Jack Lemmon
Jack Nicholson
James Cagney
James Dean: Behind the Scenes
Jane Fonda
Jeanette MacDonald & Nelson Eddy
Joan Crawford
John Wayne Films
John Wayne Reference Book
John Wayne Scrapbook
Judy Garland
Katharine Hepburn
Kirk Douglas
Laurel & Hardy
Lauren Bacall
Laurence Olivier
Mae West
Marilyn Monroe
Marlene Dietrich
Marlon Brando
Marx Brothers
Moe Howard & the Three Stooges
Norma Shearer
Olivia de Havilland
Orson Welles
Paul Newman
Peter Lorre
Rita Hayworth
Robert De Niro
Robert Redford
Sean Connery
Sexbomb: Jayne Mansfield
Shirley MacLaine
Shirley Temple
The Sinatra Scrapbook
Spencer Tracy
Steve McQueen
Three Stooges Scrapbook
Warren Beatty
W.C. Fields
William Holden
William Powell
A Wonderful Life: James Stewart

DIRECTORS

Alfred Hitchcock
Cecil B. DeMille
Federico Fellini
Frank Capra
John Huston
Steven Spielberg
Woody Allen

GENRE

Black Hollywood, Vol. 1 & 2

Classic Foreign Films: From 1960 to Today
Classic Gangster Films
Classic Science Fiction Films
Classics of the Horror Film
Classic TV Westerns
Cult Horror Films
Divine Images: Jesus on Screen
Early Classics of Foreign Film
Films of Merchant Ivory
Great Baseball Films
Great French Films
Great German Films
Great Italian Films
Great Science Fiction Films
The Great War Films
Harry Warren & the Hollywood Musical
Hispanic Hollywood
Hollywood Bedlam: Screwball Comedies
The Hollywood Western
The Incredible World of 007
The Jewish Image in American Film
The Lavender Screen: The Gay and Lesbian Films
Martial Arts Movies
The Modern Horror Film
More Classics of the Horror Film
Movie Psychos & Madmen
Our Huckleberry Friend: Johnny Mercer
Second Feature: "B" Films
They Sang! They Danced! They Romanced!
Thrillers
The West That Never Was
Words and Shadows: Literature on the Screen

DECADE

Classics of the Silent Screen
Films of the Twenties
Films of the Thirties
More Films of the 30's
Films of the Forties
Films of the Fifties
Lost Films of the 50's
Films of the Sixties
Films of the Seventies
Films of the Eighties

SPECIAL INTEREST

America on the Rerun
Bugsy (Illustrated screenplay)
The "Cheers" Trivia Book
The Citadel Treasury of Famous Movie Lines
Comic Support
Cutting Room Floor: Scenes Which Never Made It
Favorite Families of TV
Film Flubs
Film Flubs: The Sequel
Filmmaking on the Fringe
First Films
"Frankly, My Dear": Great Movie Lines About Women
The Greatest Stories Ever Filmed
Hollywood Cheesecake
Howard Hughes in Hollywood
More Character People
The Nightmare Never Ends
The "Northern Exposure" Book
The Official Andy Griffith Show Scrapbook
The 100 Best Films of the Century
The 1001 Toughest TV Trivia Questions of All Time
The "Quantum Leap" Book
Rodgers & Hammerstein
Sex in Films
Sex In the Movies
Sherlock Holmes
Son of Film Flubs
Who Is That?: Familiar Faces and Forgotten Names
"You Ain't Heard Nothin' Yet!"

For a free full-color Entertainment Books brochure including the Citadel Film Series in depth and more, call 1-800-447-BOOK; or send your name and address to Citadel Film Books, Dept. 1486, 120 Enterprise Ave., Secaucus, NJ 07094.